Badass Passive Income Ideas That Your Teacher Won't Tell You

Multiple Income Streams (Both Online And Offline) That Will Help You Achieve Financial Freedom And Money Goals

Phil C. Senior

Bluesource And Friends

This book is brought to you by Bluesource And Friends, a happy book publishing company.

Our motto is **"Happiness Within Pages"**
We promise to deliver amazing value to readers with our books. We also appreciate honest book reviews from our readers.

Connect with us on our Facebook page www.facebook.com/bluesourceandfriends and stay tuned to our latest book promotions and free giveaways.

Don't forget to claim your FREE books!

Brain Teasers:

https://tinyurl.com/karenbrainteasers

Harry Potter Trivia:

https://tinyurl.com/wizardworldtrivia

Sherlock Puzzle Book (Volume 2)

https://tinyurl.com/Sherlockpuzzlebook2

Also check out our best seller books

"67 Lateral Thinking Puzzles"

https://tinyurl.com/thinkingandriddles

"Rookstorm Online Saga"

https://tinyurl.com/rookstorm

Description

If you are looking for ways to make your money work hard for you instead of you working hard, then this book will teach you all the methods to use to make passive income.

Everyone wants to get that freedom to plan their day according to what they like doing, as opposed to planning your day based on where you need to be in order to receive your paycheck.

Or it could be that you have already taken a few relevant steps in that direction and now you want to consolidate the knowledge you have amassed and picked up a few more ideas. Whatever your starting point, by the time you complete reading this book, you will have a deeper understanding of the various passive income streams you can turn into a side hustle. You will learn a ton of passive income ideas that you can start to implement right away.

While you will learn all the ideas that starting different passive income streams it entails, I must let you know in advance that you will not be exempt from investing your time and energy. You need to know from the start that some initial effort and time has to be invested in the starting phase of any passive income business you decide to participate in.

However, the fruits of your labor will start to be seen in the years to come when your main work will be to monitor your passive income streams.

The current world has become a bit difficult to live in. One of the reasons is that our needs have doubled, and yet we cannot afford them because we don't have the money to purchase them. Well, when we open and run a passive income stream, we can be sure to generate some of the money to meet our needs.

If you have always wanted to set your own passive income stream, then keep reading.

If you want to say goodbye to your 9-5 job and do something that you are passionate about, then this book is right for you. If you don't want to make someone else rich, then this book has all the ideas and strategies to kick start your journey.

When you learn how to make passive income, there is no limit to the amount of money you can make.

With the help of this book, you will finally discover the best passive income strategies that you can start immediately to ensure that you achieve financial freedom. And this will let you take charge of your life. Whether it is that free time you want to spend or that you want to enjoy the beauty of not working for anyone, this book has everything you need to know.

Here's just a fraction of what you will learn:

- How to make money advertising on your car
- How to build a CD ladder
- How to build a network ladder
- How to make money building a forum
- How to make money publishing a book
- How to make money narrating with royalty share on ACX
- And many more…

Introduction

Most jobs we do require hard work and dedication. We deliver knowledge and labor to the company we work for to receive recognition, compensation, and satisfaction in return. Though this is a method in which we generate money, once we stop working, the income also stops flowing.

On the flipside, passive income is an idea that has been floating around the internet. The idea is that money is being earned with or without active involvement. Once it is set up, the recurring income will continue to flow.

So anyone can quickly see why this idea is very popular. Three main advantages of this idea include:

Freedom

If your passive income is higher than your cost of living, then you can free yourself from the daily cost of working for someone for at least 8 hours a day. You can enjoy your life and do whatever you want, while you continue to make enough money to support your interests.

Diversification

An alternative form of income offers diversification. An extra income is an extra layer of security for you and your family. Nothing is a guarantee in life and unexpected events may occur. A money-making opportunity can turn out to be a scam or even cause you to lose all your money.

Recurring

Passive income does not stop when you stop working. Even if we love our jobs and want to work 7 days a week, there is a time when we need to retire. At that point, the income from our jobs ends. It doesn't matter how valuable you were to the organization. If you retire, they stop paying you.

On the other hand, passive income operates even if you retire or you stop working. If you have been looking for ways to generate passive income, welcome to a comprehensive list of passive income streams.

Chapter 1: Getting Started

Is there anything sweeter than making lots of money while you are asleep? I mean, wouldn't you prefer to wake up with a large amount of cash flowing into your bank account?

Well, this concept may appear crazy, but passive income is more than just a pipe dream. According to Forbes contributor Brianna Wiest, passive income is an infinite stream of income. The point that she is trying to make is that you can never miss an opportunity.

It is said that the average millionaire has around seven different ways of earning income. Remember, that doesn't imply that they have seven jobs. But many millionaires have found a way to generate income passively.

By the time you finish reading this book, you'll be packed with great ideas on how to begin earning residual income for yourself.

The Reader's Digest reports that over 50% of Americans are instantly affected by the thoughts of work and money once they wake up in the morning.

Although earning passively besides your day job may not solve all your life challenges, it's a great place to begin, especially when you are serious about building wealth.

Passive income has been a holy grail for entrepreneurs who want to free up their time and focus on something which they are passionate about. While the significance of passive income isn't always doubted, the biggest hurdle expected is to attain a specific amount of cash flow from automatically-recurring revenue streams.

In general, it's hard to earn something from passive income. You must be ready to commit your time, and persevere at the many challenges that you will experience along the way. Sometimes, you can go for months and even years without earning a single dollar generated from passive income activities, causing even the most confident and experienced entrepreneur to shake their heads in utter frustration.

The fact is that time is far more important than money. Although money can be spent and earned, once time passes, it's gone forever. As we continue to grow older, we begin to acknowledge the significance of time and freely select what we do with those important moments that we get in life.

Chapter 2: Advertise on Your Car

Making money simply by sticking your car with an advertising wrap can be a great way to earn money if you don't care about the ads, and you fulfill the requirements.

If you qualify, you can expect to earn anywhere between $200-$400 per month just for doing what you always do, but because of auto advertising, that may mean that you drive at least 800 miles per month. For those who spend most of their time driving in busy areas and on the freeway, auto-wrap advertising can be a good means to pay for your gas.

The day Sonya Fishel Lawrence came across an online Carvertise post, she thought it was the usual scam where you receive an email offering to pay you large sums of money to put ads on your car. Lawrence thought it was too good to be true. Carvertise Inc. is a company responsible for paying drivers for pasting ads on their car.

Sonya Lawrence was looking for a means to boost her monthly salary, so this passive income idea captured her attention. She decided to do in-depth research – she read various reviews about Carverise, and finally went on to submit her application. After several weeks, the company wrapped the ad on her car and she was earning money.

Car advertisements can be a great way to earn extra income, but like any other industries, it is packed with scams. If you are looking for a means to earn money while advertising on your car, this is what you should know before you sign up:

The average American spends around 26 minutes to commute to work every day, according to a report by the Population Reference

Bureau. While you can use that time to enjoy your favorite music or even listen to audiobooks, you can still convert your commute hour into a source of money.

Companies such as Carvertise Inc. will pay drivers to put ads on their cars. Carvertise operates with local businesses to create the ads and link up with drivers in their target places. Once you are accepted as a qualified driver, the company will put colorful decals on your car for a certain time period.

The more time you spend on commute, the more you will earn while getting your car wrapped. In other words, the more you drive, the more exposure the businesses receive, so they are ready to pay some premium costs for those who cover extra miles.

Based on your commute, location, and the campaign, you can generate a revenue of between $100 to $400 per month for car-wrap advertisements.

According to Sonya, she got paid $300 at the end of the campaign. While car advertisement cannot replace your monthly earning, it's a great source of passive income because it does not demand extra time or work from you.

So, what are the steps of the car-wrap process?

Once you register for a car advertisement service, the company will ask you to provide information about your daily mileage, location, and car.

Other companies have a minimum requirement that you must fulfill. For instance, Carvertise features require a minimum of a 25-mile daily driving, and your car model should be a 2005 model or newer.

Custom paints or specialty finishes may make your vehicle ineligible, because that may affect the appearance of the car wrap. Most companies want:

- Your car to have its own factory paint job.
- As a driver, to have a clean driving record.

Once you complete your application and submit it, the company will assess your submission and check whether you are fit for an upcoming event. In some cases, the process may take weeks or even some months before you hear back from them.

In case the company selects you to help them out in their campaign, they will reach out to you and inform you of it. While you might not get the chance to select the ad that is put on your car, you can opt out if you think that the ad is inappropriate in any way.

If you decide to proceed, the company will work with you to arrange for an expert to wrap your car. The decals are used with an adhesive mostly created for vehicles so it won't destroy your paint.

This campaign can run from 1-6 months. After it's over, you may schedule an appointment with the car company to remove your decal.

Legitimate car advertising companies

Even if you do earn money advertising on your car, there are a lot of scams out there. Because of that, the Federal Trade Commission (FTC) has warned car owners about various car-wrap companies scamming consumers.

Some of these companies employ the lie that you can get paid for accepting an ad on your car only if you pay a certain fee first. Or, they may decide to send you a check for more money than they owe you and later ask you to wire them back the extra amount. Once you send back the money to them, you discover that the check was fake.

Car wrap scams are everywhere, so it's advised to research the companies thoroughly before filing any document with your personal information. If you don't know how to tell a legitimate car-wrap company from a dubious one, here are the things that you should consider:

- **They don't ask for any extra fee.** A legitimate car-wrap company will not ask drivers to pay an application fee. You need to earn money, not pay for the service.

- **They handle the wrapping cost.** Car-wrap business will pay for the cost of putting and removing the car wraps. In case they request you to cover the costs, then you should avoid this company and start to look for another company. Let them not even deceive you that they will refund you – that is another trick they may employ.

- **They have the minimum requirements set.** Scam companies don't really care about the car model you have, or if you have a bad driving history. They only want to eat your money. Authentic companies will request more information about the make of your car, year, model, and your driving record before they can approve of you.

- **You must possess car insurance.** To work with the best companies, you will need to show evidence of car insurance coverage.

- **They have a customer service line to reach out.** Say you have questions or run into some issues during a campaign, you must be able to reach out to the company and speak to a real person.

If you commute for longer hours, you can make money by just going about your daily routine. Car advertisements can be a simple way to increase your monthly income, but you must be careful before you register. Make sure you do thorough research on each company before you send in an application.

Steps to make money by advertising on your car

Registration

The first step you must do to get paid for advertising on your car is to sign up with an automotive advertising agency in your local area. Although you can get many of these companies online, you will still need a company that's near you to place the wrap on your car and remove it once the contract ends. Companies search for various things for their advertising campaigns, but the place you drive to, including your driving habits, will be a significant part of the decision process. You may also be requested to submit a good photo of your car and extra information about yourself at the time of registration.

Auto

In most cases, you don't need to have a particular type of car to have an ad wrapped on it, although some companies may only accept certain vehicles if they feel it is crucial to their message. The car has to be clean and well-painted, free of body damage and in great condition. The auto wrap is applied to your clean car, and it's up to you to maintain your car so that the advertising looks awesome. The wrap will not often destroy your paint, but if you have an old car, or are worried about your paint, make sure you ask about it before it is applied. In certain cases, damage may happen when the wrap is removed.

Contract

It is important to read the contract carefully. You should expect your advertising company to set rules on the number of miles you need to drive every month, where you will drive, and the status in which you need to maintain your car and where you must park. Companies that place advertising on automobiles tend to require the installation of certain global positioning systems (GPS) or another type of device that will record where you go and for how long you drive. You will have to meet a representative from the ad agency to download the GPS data every month before you will get paid.

Drivers

In general, auto-wrap companies have specific driver requirements to ensure their product ads only feature on cars that are driven in a safe and responsible way. The common requirements are minimum age and a clean driving record. You should also be licensed, with a clean driving record for the last 1-2 years. Typically, the advertiser will also require you to carry a higher insurance level than what the law needs.

The advantages of branding a vehicle

1. **It's an upfront, one-time cost**

One of the most interesting things about advertising a business on your car is that it is a one-time purchase. For digital ads, you will be paid for impressions garnered each day. This wrap ad is something which you will pay a fixed price for upfront and then forget about it until the time it has to be replaced.

A vinyl wrap can last for around 5 years or more, depending on the amount of care taken. Perforated window decals can also stay on for about 3 years or more with the right kind of installation and care.

On average, a wrapped vehicle is estimated to get between 600-1,000 impressions per mile driven. In a big city and on a busy road, this number is, in fact, higher. While not everyone who sees the brand will be your customer, the cost-to-exposure ratio is off the charts.

2. **No need to purchase another car**

While it makes sense for certain business owners to receive a totally different work vehicle, it might not be the right decision for you.

Although you may have to register your car as a commercial vehicle based on the state you live in, doing so would be a great way to save costs of purchasing a new vehicle. You can always consider purchasing a used fuel-efficient car if you want to maintain your business and personal assets.

3. You can become more productive

Regardless of whether you are driving to the gym or picking your kids up from school, wrapping an advertising logo and contact information on your car is the best way to turn heads and receive leads while you aren't working at your job.

Realtors, who drive in different places to showcase homes, would benefit a lot from promoting their name simultaneously. You can be productive and kill two birds with one stone while driving every day.

The disadvantages of advertising

1. Sometimes, it may not be legal to brand your car

Based on the place where you live in, it may be prohibited to advertise on your car. For instance, if your state restricts rear-tinted windows, it is possible that you would be unable to use some or all the methods of advertising on your rear window.

First, you must examine your state's law. Perform some research and confirm with your local DMV for information associated with vehicle restrictions. You may also have to re-register the family truck as a commercial vehicle if you use it to promote your business. Besides that, you have to separate your business insurance policy from a personal one. To avoid the fines and tickets, it's important to get the details squared off first.

You may also need to consider your city laws because it is not unusual for mobile advertisements to be restricted.

In case you have a Homeowners' Association, you may have to ensure that your car is permitted to be parked on your driveway. Some residential facilities may not permit entry to vehicles that are covered with advertisements. Failure to stick by these rules may lead to your car getting towed as a result. Thus, you need to save yourself the hassle beforehand and seek your attorney for legal advice first.

2. You will often be representing the business

If you get the rear window graphics installed on your personal vehicle, you will be representing the company in the ads.

Choosing to speed and road rage in a vehicle that advertises the designated company will destroy your mobile marketing efforts. You will need to be aware of how you conduct yourself, and how your car appears. You might have to go for car washes more often to maintain the trunk of the car organized and vacuumed.

Of course, there is the possibility of lawsuits. Don't allow that to affect you, but there are many ways to prepare your business and secure your assets. Consult your lawyer if you want legal advice.

3. It can make your friends or clients feel uncomfortable

Depending on your choice of work, it can make your friends feel uncomfortable when your branded car is parked outside their house.

For instance, if you are a marriage counselor, your client may not want his or her friends to know that they are experiencing some family challenges.

It is vital to confirm with your clients first to know that they feel comfortable with your car parked outside of their house. You can always park down the street, but if you have a street van with many tools and equipment, this will make your work more difficult.

That said, it is good to respect the privacy of your friends and clients.

Chapter 3: Affiliate Marketing

Affiliate marketing is one of the best ways to make passive income online. If you have ever thought of making money while sleeping, then affiliate marketing is one of those techniques that will help you to realize that dream.

In the United Kingdom, affiliate marketing contributes to around 1% of the country's GDP, based on research done from IAB UK. That is more than the whole agriculture industry.

The same research indicates that affiliate marketers in the UK generate £15 for every £1 they use and it's easy to understand why many people dive into the industry with that level of return on investment (ROI) on the table.

But don't think that affiliate marketing is a get-rich-quick scheme. Like anything worth doing in this world, affiliate marketing is a tricky venture, but with the right plan in place, you can enter the list of entrepreneurs who find success in affiliate marketing.

By definition, affiliate marketing can be described as a performance-based marketing technique in which a retailer rewards a website with a small commission for every customer referred through the website's marketing activities. The website will only get paid when the marketing leads to a transaction.

Typically, affiliate marketing involves a retailer that pays a small commission to affiliates who suggest their products or services to others.

In most instances, this requires sending traffic to a retailer's website and then receiving a commission when the visitors purchase the product they are recommending.

There are usually four parties in this procedure:

The merchant: This is the company that sells the product or service.

The affiliate: The person that markets the service or product.

Affiliate networks: Online networks from which merchants list affiliate programs and where affiliates can find them.

The consumer: These are the people that affiliates recommend services/products to, and finally end up buying them from the merchant.

Affiliate networks are optional. So if you are an affiliate, you don't have to use them to run a successful program and merchants don't have to use them to identify affiliates. However, they can still be useful to both parties in certain situations.

The merchants are interested in optimizing sales of their products or services. With affiliate marketing, they can ask other people to market for them and only have to pay a small commission when a person purchases from them.

With a huge network of affiliates marketing their services/products, merchants can gain a valuable source of traffic and sales. It is like a win-win plan for the merchants because they only pay when sales occur.

Similarly, the costs of affiliate marketing are a fraction of what merchants pay per conversion via pay-per-click (PPC) and all of the time-consuming aspects of content creation.

What do affiliates receive from this?

Affiliates earn a small commission every time the services or products that they recommend are purchased. The main benefit here is that you can generate money without the need to build your own products. All the hard tasks have already been done by the merchants whom you partner up with.

This doesn't mean that you win a free ride as an affiliate. You will need to build and control your website, develop a continuous stream of great content and generate sufficient traffic to ensure that your affiliate venture is profitable.

Since you will be earning a small commission for each sale, you will have to secure a huge volume of customers for your partner merchants to pay for your effort, time and initial costs. Then you can generate sufficient profit on top of that.

What is the responsibility of affiliate networks?

Affiliate networks are online platforms where merchants get a chance to advertise their affiliate programs to attract an affiliate.

You don't need to use networks to participate in affiliate marketing, though. You will discover a lot of businesses that market their programs openly on their website and you can register with them directly.

But networks can boost the process, and some merchants prefer to work with them exclusively to include a layer of security to their program.

It's all about the consumers

"Consumers" refer to users who really need to purchase from the merchant's website. For this to take place, the affiliate should target them with the right content, prove to them that the merchant is worth buying from, and then send them to the merchant's website where they can complete the process.

Not everyone will be interested in whatever product the merchant wants to sell, so the ability of the affiliate to create visits from people with a great interest in the merchant's offer and a massive purchase intention is important.

How affiliate marketing operates

Now that you have an idea of the basics, let's look closely at how affiliate marketing operates.

Affiliate marketing payment models

In most instances, affiliates earn a commission when one or more of their visitors scans through a merchant's website and buys one of their products. But there are other affiliate marketing models you may come across:

Pay-Per-Sale (PPS): The affiliate will be paid for each sale they generate. This is the common model because it shifts all the responsibility and risk to the affiliate.

Pay-Per-Lead (PPL): The affiliate is paid for each lead created: Trial creations, online form submissions, free demo signups, or any pre-purchase.

Pay-Per-Click (PPC): In this model, the affiliate is paid for all traffic/clicks generated, whether the visitors turn into leads or customers. This model is rare, and all the risks rest with the merchant.

Most affiliate programs implement the PPS model, which implies that you will only get paid when your referral traffic purchases the product or the service you recommend.

Monitoring the traffic of affiliate marketing

No matter the type of affiliate program model you register to, merchants need the means to learn where traffic is originating from. Any merchant can have hundreds, thousands, or even millions of affiliates and only the ones accountable for each sale will be paid.

Well, how does this operate?

You register to an affiliate program and you are provided with a unique ID, which you can add to the end of all your links for the program.

When are you paid?

This will depend on the affiliate programs you use and you will want to ensure that you know your stand before you register anything.

In general, merchants will pay out either on a monthly or weekly basis.

If you use an affiliate network, then the rules can be different. Most of them feature payout thresholds, which means that you can withdraw money only when you hit a certain amount in your balance. Typically, this threshold is low so it shouldn't be a problem.

What expenses do affiliate marketers need to pay?

The first expense will be creating a website. This website is where you will post your content and make your recommendations, as well as develop your audience. This is going to involve the following things:

- Domain name
- Hosting
- Development costs
- Web design
- Website maintenance

This will allow you to get your website to run, but you will still need to invest your money and time in creating content that influences buyers' purchasing decisions.

You will also require a website in case the content will generate traffic and thus affiliate income. PPC, Search Engine Optimization, social media, and other inbound marketing methods require time and money.

You will want to invest in strategies that make the best of your traffic. This may include conversion optimization, email marketing, and UX testing.

It is critical to know what your expenses are so that you can make an accurate plan and stick to it.

Step-by-Step: Affiliate Marketing

Though affiliate marketing is a straightforward idea, the process used to implement a strategy can be quite difficult. Below is a quick look at what you'll require to become an affiliate marketer.

Plan: Any successful affiliate marketing strategy begins with comprehensive planning.

Develop your site: Develop your website, build your domain, and define your niche.

Set up analytics: Build analytics and determine your KPIs so that you can measure and boost performance.

Select your programs: Select affiliate content that recommends services/ products you have signed up with.

Grow your audience: Market your content, develop your search engine presence and generate sufficient traffic so that you can make some affiliate income.

Attain profitability: Build it into your affiliate marketing plan that you are earning more than you pay for and it is sufficient to cover the time you invest.

Optimize performance: Maximize your website and strategy to make the most out of your traffic and affiliate programs.

Scale the strategy: Try out new methods to expand your audience and double your affiliate revenue.

Automate everything you can: Optimize your profits while minimizing the manual workload.

That is the path you will take to ensure you are a successful affiliate marketer.

Becoming an affiliate marketer

For you to become successful as an affiliate marketer, you will need the following:

- A collection of products to review and recommend within your regular content.
- Platforms where you can suggest these products.
- A large audience to enable you to make sufficient income as an affiliate.

- An affiliate marketing method to optimize profit.

Planning your way to affiliate marketing

If you throw yourself into affiliate marketing with a general idea of what you want to do but have a dull attitude, you will fall out of love with this game fast.

Unfortunately, this seems to be the way most people approach things.

The good thing is that you are not going to make the same mistake. You will need to plan things out carefully, set annual targets for the first three years, divide them down into achievable monthly targets and accurately predict the money and time you need to invest to receive the results.

First, you will need to do the following:

- Identify the budget you are working with
- Know how much your website is going to cost
- Know how much your content will cost
- Know the amount you are going to spend on advertising
- Know the amount of money you will spend on marketing tools
- Understand the amount of profit you need to make
- Understand how much you are going to make from every affiliate sale
- Understand the amount of traffic you need to send to partner sites to achieve your sales target

- Understand the amount of traffic you need to achieve on your own platforms to send sufficient traffic to partner sites and realize your sales targets

Once you have your plan organized, combine your plan with your yearly and monthly targets. Ensure that your numbers add up and confirm that there is sufficient budget to achieve your goals.

Find products that you want to market

Now it's time to select the products you want to market in your affiliate marketing plan. With many different choices out there, it can be confusing to scale them down, but you must choose a strategic plan for selecting the correct products.

Market products you already know and love

In general, you should consider marketing products you already know and have enthusiasm for. Don't attempt to recommend web design software to expert designers if you have never designed a site yourself. You cannot manage to speak about the product in more detail to make genuine suggestions.

However, you can look to your personal and professional life: What kind of software do you use daily? What kind of products do you know inside-out that others find it hard to understand? What are your biggest passions in life?

It might be something simple, such as accounting software that you use at work. You know it inside-out, you know why you hate it, and this provides you with sufficient knowledge to try alternative softwares and make a judgment on what makes them better than others.

Affiliate marketing scales down to having sufficient knowledge about the services and products you promote, to assist less-informed people to make right buying decisions. Or, at least, make people feel as if they are making the right purchasing decisions.

We're discussing business owners who hate their accounting software but don't want to try 10 options to find the best one. Or photographers who want to purchase the right camera, but don't know where to begin.

Your responsibility as an affiliate marketer is to assist people to make purchasing decisions – and the commissions are your reward.

Actively look for products in your niche

Once you choose what your niche is going to be, you can begin to select products to market. You need to have a list of possible products in mind, and you can look at their website directly to see whether they have an affiliate strategy.

If it does, add it to the list of possible options.

If they don't, then you will not earn any profit from suggesting products, but you can still apply the knowledge you have about them into your content.

Once you determine which of your products do/don't have affiliate plans, it's time to look for alternative options.

Chapter 4: Be a Narrator with Royalty Share on ACX

Have you ever been told that you have a nice voice? Whether or not you have already undertaken professional speaking lessons, you can generate money doing voice-overs. All you need is a clear and attractive voice.

So what does an audiobook narrator involve?

When you consider voice-over acting, you may think of the talented voices behind animated movies and the stiff competition in the industry. This doesn't mean that this will always be the case. Still, people like you and me can become successful as voice-over actors.

The best way to start is by narrating audiobooks. In recent years, audiobooks have increased in popularity. One reason is that people are becoming busier and carry their phones around with them all the time – thus, they prefer to listen to books rather than read them on their devices.

As a narrator of the audiobook, you'll be converting print and digital books into audio files by reading them in your great voice.

Things you need to get started

The basic things that you must have to get started as an audiobook narrator include:

- Voice training

- A record of your voice

- A PC to manage your work and upload recordings

- Headphones
- A voice-over microphone and microphone stand
- Recording software, like Audacity
- Hide any regional accents, or at least overcome them
- Take part in voice lessons
- Pop filters to block the initial popping and breathing when a mouth first interacts with the microphone

It will possibly depend on how committed you want to be, and whether or not the devices you will be using will be supplied to you. One way is to rent a recording studio to perform your own demo tapes, or even do some fair bit of recording yourself. This can be a bit expensive, because many recording studios charge on a per hour basis.

Where can you find freelance work as an audiobook narrator?

If you have ever tried to search for freelance work on any of the bidding sites: Upwork, Freelancer, Guru.com and Fiverr, amongst others, then you have possibly seen voice-over artists there marketing their skills. No big deal, given the number of eBooks that are out there, too.

But, there are two websites specially focused on audiobook narration work:

- **ACX.com:** On the following website, you will receive opportunities to link up with authors looking for voice-over artists for audiobooks and eBooks. Also, ACX assists both authors and narrators in their marketing efforts on social media and offline, too. There are extra opportunities to find and maximize agents for your talent and earn royalties both as an author and voice-over artist. There is a simple search tool on the site that makes it easy to find posted jobs.

- **Voices.com:** This site was developed by Stephanie Ciccarelli, who has trained in voice, musical theatre, and piano. The site provides useful advice for both audiobook authors and voice-over artists. Although this site does have job postings, it appears to be mainly focused on helping one learn to discover their clients and maintain up-to-date with industry news.

How much can you generate doing voice-over work?

This one depends on how well you are known, including your experience and portfolio. In addition, you will have to pay attention to the sound quality of your voice overs before you send them.

On sites such as freelance bidding sites and Fiverr.com, you might not generate sufficient money when you start out, but you will slowly develop your experience and portfolio. The normal rates for most freelance work are $20 -$33 per hour.

How can you launch a freelance career doing voice-overs and narrations?

As required, you must do your homework and decide whether this is something you want to do. Although it takes some time to develop a freelancing career, this one requires a person to set up a recording studio with their own equipment if they want to do it professionally from their own house. That may run up some amount of money.

But, if after considering all options, you are still interested in the entire idea of recording audiobook narrations, then proceed.

The four metrics to succeed as an ACX Audiobook producer

One of my closest friends is a highly successful audiobook narrator with different years of experience working in commercial studios for traditional publishers. I have discussed with him about using ACX, including things such as:

- The ease of getting interesting books on the site and auditioning to narrate them

- The potential to work directly with authors and fill holes in the recording schedule

- The possibility of building one's own publishing company and working on titles of one's choice in spare time

- The excitement of earning passive income at the end of every month from carefully selected Royalty Share projects

Additionally, traditional publishers will go for narrators experienced in home recording.

Once he was confident that building a home recording studio would be a great career move on all levels, he decided to build one and ask questions while implementing the strategy.

That said, here are four things that new home recording users working via ACX may benefit from:

1. **An efficient recording software**

Your choice of computer systems and Digital Audio Workstation softwares are critical. You can go for a proprietary, self-contained system – this one doesn't need you to learn how to use a recording software. However, it is important to select software that many of your peers also use so that you can easily train and get support.

You should also consider the needs of your clients and even find out what some of their main publishers use.

The choice of your software may not be so clear-cut, and, therefore, you must do detailed research to learn the pros and cons of your chosen software.

Before you start doing an ACX project, you must learn how to use the software – at least master the basic skills of recording, saving and exporting files. As a narrator, you must realize that on-going training in audiobook performance is vital throughout your career.

2. Work habits

Once you complete your software training, then you should develop good habits and practices in the home studio to ensure that your workflow is in line with traditional audiobook publishers'.

One of the most critical things that a narrator can do to enhance the recording process is to master the "punch-and-roll" recording technique.

Traditional audiobook publishers finish recording a book before editing it. That way, if you want to change anything in the book, it will not need to be edited twice.

New narrators will learn a lot concerning sound quality and narration ability by listening to their own voice while improving the audio files.

Because you can narrate another book while the first one is being edited, it is better to outsource your narration for editing and proofreading as much as possible. You can request your narrator friends to tell you about editor recommendations, or get in touch with people who have listed their services and rates.

Regardless of whether you are working as an editor, editing your own audio or building your files, you need to develop a file-naming convention for your recordings. The correct format for the naming convention isn't important as long as the names are clear and consistent. It's also good to include a book title in the section name.

3. Communication

Audiobook narration is a special art that depends on the narrator's interpretation of the author's words. The job of the voice-over actor is to make choices in the whole performance. The choices will not often match the choices the rights holder (RH) would make. As a result, it is important to set expectations at the outset.

Unless the RH is ready to pay per real-time hour to direct you through each second of the whole performance, you need to communicate clearly on the types of revisions you will accept when a project ends.

You should also discuss the rate and due dates of any product before you accept an offer. Once you confer with the RH about your availability and the amount of time required for the production, you can set dates with the editor and notify the RH of the due dates.

4. Paperwork

No work is finished until when all the paperwork is done. Most of the ACX producer's paperwork involves payment and tax issues.

You will have to invoice the RH for a "pay-for-production" project. In the case of stipend project, the stipend is paid by ACX.

The challenge of audiobook narration

In particular, working via ACX demands that you do the production yourself – that is editing and mastery of the process. So, there is a technical learning curve.

Audiobooks demand hours and hours of editing other than voice-over work.

You can consider starting small, especially if you are new.

Look online for voice-over jobs and you will come across marketing videos under five minutes.

But still, online course videos will demand some hours of voice-over. Grow your skills on smaller tasks and work your way up to bigger projects.

While you can outsource the work to an audio editor, that is probably not worth it for an audiobook.

Outsourcing the work will cut into your pay, so it is better to learn to do everything yourself.

Some tips that you can consider include:

- Avoid page-turning noises
- Turn off any Wi-Fi connections from devices and set them to *Airplane mode* to avoid static noises.
- Every ACX file has to be a single chapter of a book. It is easier to record these as separate files instead of cutting them up later.

Chapter 5: Book Publishing

Many people want to publish a novella, short story, or a full-fledged novel, but the challenges of traditional publishing can be very high. In particular, if you are a new author without any experience, it is difficult to get started and engage a large audience. Fortunately, the self-publishing industry offers a different pathway to publishing.

First, you must learn how to market yourself, with a course bundle that will teach you how to develop a responsive website, including how to build a Gravatar, look for a hosting package and create your own domain name. It is vital to understand the nitty-gritty of using your website, especially when you don't have a publisher to assist you. You must know how to install WordPress, configure basic settings and discover the right plug-ins for your site. You will learn how to make your content visible and develop your own library of books that are accessible to your readers online.

Next, you must learn about Kindle publishing. This is a plus because it is the world's largest book marketplace. Be introduced to the steps behind Kindle Direct Publishing, as this will assist you to publish your book on Amazon.com, promote your book, research competitors, and many more. You will learn from your competition, learn how to create top-selling descriptions and set up the prices of your books via KDP. Still, you can get a course that will teach you how to build eye-catching cover art to market to the readership, and how you can source for images for marketing purposes.

There's still a particular formatting guideline for Kindle because poor formatting can turn readers away. You must learn to use Scrivener to format Kindle books properly and provide your readers with a professional, enjoyable reading experience.

You can even look for a course that deals with how to use a Scrivener tool because it does have some sort of a learning curve. You will encounter important productivity tips and practices that you can apply in your Scrivener experience – this include best practices to write, outline, edit and rewrite.

Dispelling the author myth

Many people assume that there are two kinds of authors when it comes to making money as a book publisher: The best-selling authors who earn millions of dollars in their publishing contract, and struggling authors who earn little income even after a family member purchases the copy.

The truth is, there is no fixed amounts of money you can guess because there are many factors that determine the potential income of an author. There are a few authors who generate millions and many more that cannot hit the $500 threshold, and even lose money.

As an author, it is your responsibility to know how much you can earn from your hard work. For some people, simply publishing a book is enough. Others may not care about earning such cash for their words.

The first step should be to learn how to make that cash. As an author, there are two basic methods you can use to generate money, from book sales or things you sell relating to the contents of your book.

1. **Direct book sales**

Authors generate money from their book sales in two methods: An advance or royalties. An advance is money that is handed to the author from a publishing company before the book is released. Advances are often given to authors who have a nice record of publishing best-selling books, or have a high possibility of becoming a best-seller. Only those authors who have a publishing contract can receive advances.

Both the self-published and traditionally published authors can receive royalties. Royalties refer to money given to an author once a book is published and sold. Authors earn a portion of the sale based on how they publish their book. If you work with a publishing company, a percentage of the royalties has to go to the publisher, an agent, and then to you. In case you are a self-published author, you will need to pay the company that helped you to get your book published. However, you get a higher percentage back.

Another method to earn money on direct book sales is to develop books in different formats such as hardback, paperback, digital, audio, etc. This will assist you to meet a different audience from a format that they are more comfortable with.

2. Sales determined by the content of your book

Authors search for income opportunities beyond selling books. The main reason for this is the limited sales capacity of a book. Once you sell a book, the transaction ends until the time when an author creates another book. But in case an author sells things based on the book content, that author has multiple ways of earning income.

Here are examples:

- Pre-sales
- Travel tours/ special events
- Teaching in their writing style
- Products based on the content

Creative methods to generate money from your book

1. Sell coffee mugs, T-shirts, or market items using characters from your book on your personal website, or even through sites like Zazzle, CafePress, etc., if you are crafty.
2. Create crowdfunding campaigns on sites such as Indiegogo, Inc., to generate money for expenses that you cannot manage.
3. Sell exclusive bonus material like poems, chapters, and short stories via websites.
4. Offer a fiction-writing course in your selected non-profit topics.

Book promotion ideas that work

Unless you are a celebrity best-selling author, traditional publishers expect you to do most of the heavy-lifting when it comes to marketing your book. Regardless of what you are writing, if you want to make good money, you will have to learn the marketing tips on your own.

Many authors get confused when they want to market their book, and hence they employ a PR person to pitch and market their books to media outlets. This section will take you through some of the tips before you go out to employ any PR professional. You will discover that some of the book-marketing can be done by yourself, and you will be saving a lot of time and money on the ones that you would otherwise be delegating.

Know that you are in the marketing business and not the authoring business

This is vital before you sit down to write the first word. When you consider being a marketer first, and then an author or writer second, you will instantly put your focus on what matters – your audience, the challenges they are trying to solve and how you can assist them to solve those challenges.

The same is true for fiction writers – John Locke, who has sold over a million books on Amazon and earned more than a million dollars by selling $.99 eBooks did exactly this way.

He discovered that many successful authors were selling books for $10 per book, and decided to undercut them by selling his books at $.99.

Locke had a good foundation about business techniques and considered carefully who his right audience was, how they spent their days, and things that frustrated them, including the type of content they would likely consume.

This was not an easy process as you may think, because he had his trial-and-error times.

Develop a simple marketing plan for your content

Maybe you are asking yourself why you need to do this when you plan to employ a marketing expert to perform this for you. You need to do this by yourself so that you can select the right marketing/PR person who will assist you to generate money from your book.

With this plan in place, you will be ready to begin playing around with some specific marketing plans to generate money from your writing.

Develop a video trailer: A book is nothing more than a movie you play in your mind – develop a video trailer to allow people to be interested in the book. You can use tools such as Animoto, Magisto, or Adobe Spark.

Build a Facebook group or fan page: Build a space where your fans, audience, and potential readers can interact with you.

Develop a website: You can write a simple book or author website on your own for lower than $100. Invest in a better design, book image, images, and headshots. In addition, provide free content like table of contents, a specific chapter, or even develop a series of downloadable resources and tools for your audience.

These items are just a tip of the iceberg to help authors understand how to leverage their content and have different options. As an author, you aren't limited to staying around and waiting for your book to generate money for you. You can make use of your book's content to generate opportunities for even more money. The only limits would be your imagination and time.

Things you should learn from book publishing

1. **Publishers look for audiences and not authors**

When publishers search for new authors, the first thing they consider is a person with an audience. Publishers don't throw a lot of money into marketing a book unless it is selling. Whether or not the book sells depends on the ability of the author to sell it.

If you want to be published but don't have an audience, the best thing you can do is to begin blogging. This will develop your audience and confirm whether or not you are a great writer.

2. **Big individuals use ghostwriters**

Here's why big authors don't write their own books.

- They don't have time. One way that you can save yourself time is to let another person create the book for you.

- Big-time authors aren't good writers. They feature influential insights and can communicate the excellent ideas as speakers, but they tend to struggle to put the same ideas into writing.

In most cases, a ghostwriter can write and communicate the same ideas better than the author, generating a quality book.

3. **70% don't make a profit**

Jenkins Group is a top publishing firm that released a report that 70% of books don't make a profit. When people create a joke about the cover designer making it better than the author's work, it's usually the case.

If you are yet to decide whether self-publishing is the best option for you, there's an educative course that asks critical questions to assist you to make your decision and defines for you the four main financial investments that self-published authors can make. You can find an online course that will assist you in dealing with the most prominent problems that writers experience – this will help you outline a planning idea to make sure that you write often, and may include tricks to assist you to stay ahead of the curve in your particular genre.

Chapter 6: Build a Network Marketing Team

In good times and bad, people are continuously focusing on network marketing as a main source of income.

How to generate money in network marketing is something that every new network marketer wants to know.

The network marketing sector is packed with resourceful information on how one can make money. But still, there is always a group of people who think that there's an easier route to making money.

There are different reputable network marketing operations, but some have been defined as "pyramid" schemes. The latter may choose to concentrate on sales to consumers rather than the employment of salespeople, who may need to pay for expensive starter kits.

How network marketing operates

Network marketing is defined by different names, including: Cellular marketing, multi-level marketing or even affiliate marketing.

Companies that adhere to a network marketing model normally build tiers of salespeople. In other words, salespeople are encouraged to hire their own networks of salespeople. The developers of a new tier make a commission on their own sales and sales generated by individuals roped into the tier they build. With time, a new tier can emerge, and another one too, which leads to more commission to the person in the top tier.

As a result, the earnings of salespeople depend on recruitment. Those who join early belong to the top tier – which makes the most.

Pros and cons of network marketing

There is a certain perception linked to network marketing – in particular, those with multiple tiers can be described as "pyramid" schemes. The salesperson in the top tier can generate huge amounts of money on commissions from the tiers below them. Those at the lower tiers will earn less. The company generates money by selling expensive starter kits to new employees.

The interesting part of network marketing is that a person with sufficient energy and great sales skills can build a profitable business using a modest investment.

A good rule of thumb based on the Federal Trade Commission (FTC) is that single-tier network marketing operations tend to be more reputable than multi-tier schemes, where people generate money depending on the number of distributors they recruit.

The attraction of network marketing is that a person with more energy and great sales skills can generate more significant business with a good investment.

According to the Federal Trade Commission (FTC), a single-tier network marketing operations appears to be more reputable than a multi-tier scheme, in which people generate money based on the number of distributors they hire.

Some great examples of single-tier network marketing operations consist of: Avon Products, Excel Communications, and Mary Kay, amongst others.

Making money with network marketing

The sales agent will not only make money from selling the products of the company, but there is still a great probability to generate money using network marketing via developing a large down line. A member will make a specific percentage from the sale to a person he recruits. In line with the following, it is important that the hierarchy is a structure where the sales agent is "built up" and the individual who recorded the most active sales agent under him has the possibility to generate a significant amount of cash for a long time via residual income. Many people know a person who participates in network marketing. While it is not that popular in Europe, it is great business in the United States. In fact, it is approximated that network marketing accounts for more than $50 billion in sales alone, so there is basically a large amount of money to be generated from this business model. Before you sign up to a network marketing business, it is important to consider whether the company you are working with is actually legitimate. Understand that there is a big difference between a pyramid scheme and an authentic multi-level networking company.

You need to participate in a genuine company to experience the long-term benefits from this business. Also, understand that pyramid schemes are illegal, so you must stay as far away from those as possible. Once you sign up for a network marketing business, you will basically conclude that it offers a win-win situation for the parent company and the network marketers. The reason is that it offers the company a great opportunity to generate their product to the market without depending on retail establishments which give support to massive multi-national companies over smaller companies. Similarly, the network marketers will reap benefits for themselves rather than be given a trade margin like traditional retailers – the company can take advantage of their membership and offer them a percentage from their sales.

Many people make a mistake of forcing their relatives and family members to join their network marketing company. You need to know that it is not right to force anyone if they are not interested in the opportunity. This may affect the relationship between you and your family or friends.

There are a lot of markets that you can tap into especially today, where you can market your network marketing business over the internet. Creating your down line should not be a rigorous exercise. There are a lot of online selling methods you can take advantage of, such as viral marketing, email campaigns, and even pay-per-click (PPC) advertising. You can expect huge results from using these methods, especially when you carefully plan your marketing campaign. Apart from that, you can still make use of traditional marketing methods such as newspaper advertising, releasing leaflets and magazine advertisements. You can also market your business in exhibitions, trade shows, and other business events. Still, today, many people use all these techniques to become successful in their network marketing business. You can still apply these methods to generate money using network marketing.

Sales tips to generate money with network marketing

1. **Run competitions**

People like to compete, and they love incentives.

So, you must be creative. Set up a 30-day challenge or a contest for a goal you would want to attain – like generating more sales. For instance, you can set up a 5-day sales contest. Think of an incentive: It can be a one-on-one coaching call or a gift card, and even a trip to an interesting destination. Brainstorm with your team members, and you might be surprised.

2. **Be prepared**

Be aware of the most important dates and how you can use it to your advantage.

During the holidays, most companies run many promotions. That is great news. You need to share it with your team and teach them how to pre-plan so that you can optimize the promotions.

3. Create unique packages

Suppose you have built special packages of products for your customers? Those are interesting to talk about and market. This will allow your customers and prospects to get started and also refer their friends.

If you want to attain massive results, you need to change your mindset. It's no longer about you, but about the people that you help out. How can you make it interesting?

Chapter 7: Build a CD (Certificates of Deposit) Ladder

Most people who save desire to earn as much income as they can from their savings. If you can lock up your money for a specific period of time, then a CD can be a great way to earn a higher interest rate from your bank. Opening a CD isn't hard, but easy, what with many banking institutions available. In addition, you will receive a different variety of terms and rates to fulfill your needs.

One method to receive income from your savings is to apply a "CD ladder" method. To employ this method, you'll need to open different CD accounts with various dates of maturity. This will allow you to maximize the higher rates that many banks provide on longer-term CDs without the security of every penny of your money for an extended period of time. Below, is a comprehensive look at CD ladders and how you may create a plan that will work for you.

The basics of CDs

If you open a certificate of deposit account, you are definitely extending a loan to your bank. You accept to deposit your cash with the bank for a fixed time period. In return, your bank will agree to pay you a specific interest at certain intervals, and then provide you with your whole principal investment when the CD grows.

You can actually get CDs that will provide terms of different lengths of time you like. Some CDs will grow in less than a month, while you can sometimes identify CDs with terms featuring 10 years or even longer. Approximately, all banks will present you with options for CDs ranging from 3-5 years, with numerous choices in between.

In most cases, the longer the maturity rates of a CD, the higher the rate of the CD. Recently, the difference between 1-year CD rates and 5-year CD rates has been approximately half a percentage point. Before this, this difference was larger, sometimes attaining a full percentage point. This difference may not appear big, but on a $10,000 CD, receiving an extra half percentage point means $50 extra income per year.

How CD ladders operate

Typically, you will want to earn the highest rates that long-term CDs present, but you may not want to lock up your savings for that time period. If you want instant access to a certain amount of your savings, then a CD ladder can offer you the best of both worlds.

In particular, a CD-ladder approach allows you to own different CDs that meet your cash and income needs. When getting started with a CD ladder, you will need to purchase CDs with different maturity terms. It is normal to set up the same amounts into each CD, as most people have cash needs that are consistent over time. Some prefer to apply a certain amount of their savings toward opening CDs, and then add on further CD accounts to offer more financial flexibility.

Let's find out how that works in normal life: In this case, you want to invest
$100,000 at the start of 2019. Your bank will pay you 2.5% on a 1-year CD, 2.75% on a 4-year CD, and 3% on a 5-year CD. To create a bond ladder immediately, you can open around five CD accounts for $20,000 each, with a maturity in 2020, 2021, 2022, 2023, and 2024.

Similarly, if you want to spread out your cash, you can invest $25,000 of your $100,000 total now, open a five $5,000 CDs. Then 3 months from now, you can do the same thing, and do the same every three months until the time you invest all your cash in CDs. The final result would be 20 CDs of $5,000 each, with one CD-striking due every quarter between early 2020 and late 2024.

Why CD ladders are better

CD ladders have two significant advantages: They optimize your long-term interest, and they offer you constant access to a certain amount of your cash. Take into consideration the simple five-CD bond ladder above. It generates an average of 2.75% in interest, which is above the 2.5% provided on a single-year CD. Yet it provides you access to the $20,000 in savings in the one-year CD as early as 2020. If you have made the necessary arrangements, then having that huge access should fulfill your anticipated financial needs.

If you want to spend money on the maturing CD, then you basically withdraw it and avoid any penalty for withdrawing early. However, the genuine strength of the CD ladder starts when you reinvest that money. The next thing in the CD-ladder strategy is to reinvest any growing CD in the longest term of the ladder.

CD ladders can be a smart strategy for savers. It can be very important in a rising-rate environment. If you are searching for a low-risk investment but want to take advantage of the increasing rates, CD ladders can be a great consideration.

For a fixed-rate, CDs are basically low-to-no-risk propositions. CD laddering lets you gain access to your cash in specific intervals and you can use that money for something different.

Whether you don't like to risk or you are in a state where you know you are going to demand access to money within a specific time frame, a CD ladder can be a great option.

Why CD ladder isn't the best

The fact is that the CD ladder isn't perfect for every situation. If you are looking for a method to invest money in the long run, then you can earn better profit by applying aggressive tactics to other investments such as stocks. CDs are secured from principal loss, so they are important for short-term needs, but if you really think that you can continue to reinvest your CD ladder indefinitely, then it is more sensible to search for stock alternatives to improve your general returns.

Additionally, if you need money on a schedule that is not the same with the way you have set up a CD ladder, then you may end up paying early-withdrawal penalties. Depending on the bank you choose, that can cost you months or even a year or more in interest – a costly mistake that you will want to avoid if you can.

Another thing to keep in mind while purchasing CDs from banks, is that they might not always have your best interests in mind.

So you need to be alert as CDs mature, because banks have aggressive sales methods and they might attempt to recommend you to speak to someone who isn't a certified financial planner. Understanding that you have money in hand from your new matured CD, the salesperson for the bank may attempt to sell you something else which you don't want.

Chapter 8: Buy Existing Online Businesses

To own and run an online business doesn't imply that you have to create a business from scratch. Most entrepreneurs do so because they have sufficient time, energy and skills, but other alternatives exist as well. If you want to manage an online business but want to quickly achieve the benefits of huge traffic, profit, and customers, then you should consider buying an existing business for sale.

Buying versus beginning a new online business

What purchasing an online business for sale implies comes down to eliminating the time, money and knowledge investment needed to develop a business from scratch while reaping the advantages of owning an online business.

Purchasing a business assists entrepreneurs to move past the introductory stages of developing a startup, such as the long hours, restricted cash flow, system establishment, inventory sourcing, traffic and customer generation.

When entrepreneurs purchase an online business, they have the opportunity to invest in a company that is already proven to be profitable. Additionally, the products are in demand, which is a great asset. Entrepreneurs can buy into existing businesses to attain a bigger share of the market in an industry that they already exist in, making them a tougher competitor and providing them with a huger chance to dominate the market.

Even if purchasing an online business for sale seems like a greater idea than launching a new business from scratch, it is still critical to consider all the pros and cons that come with it.

Although it may appear like an easier and faster passage to success than developing a new brand from scratch, there can still be risks. The upfront investment when purchasing an online business for sale is definitely bigger than starting a business from scratch – you might need to take over inefficient processes and systems, you might take on existing employees, and there could be possible liabilities and legal risks applied to the business. As a result, doing your own due diligence is the most critical thing if you want to buy an online business for sale.

Why is an online business a great investment?

When you purchase an online business for sale, you will be putting yourself in the position to invest in online property the same way that you invest in physical property such as real estate.

Online business such as the digital version of physical property can expand and succeed over time. The "space" digital assets such as online businesses occupy are valuable, and by purchasing this property, it will lead to huge profits later.

Apart from owning valuable digital property, there are many reasons why online business for sale can be a great investment. An online business can generate passive income. In other words, for low hourly input, they can lead to a higher monetary result. They can still be run besides the routine 9-5 job, implying that the owner and operator of the business make additional income apart from their normal salary. Purchasing an online business for sale can be easy if you shop around in a few marketplaces.

Owning an online business for sale can be as hands-off as you want the process to be, but either way, buying an online business for sale can be a great asset to make a huge profit on. This can enable you to earn income passively while you go about your daily work.

Pros and cons of purchasing an online business for sale

Purchasing an online business for sale and beginning a business from scratch both have their own advantages and disadvantages – that is the reason why neither is better than the other. Therefore, it is critical to know the advantages and disadvantages before you choose to commit to either one.

Advantages of purchasing an online business for sale

- **The legal work is already done**: You can decide to go past the nights and hours needed to begin a business from scratch. Somebody has done that for you already.

- **The business is up and running already:** There is no need to launch a strategy and implement launch campaigns – the business has already gone past that stage.

- **The customer base is already established:** You won't waste time to work on creating initial traffic to the online business – a customer base already exists that buys from the store.

- **You can go straight into growing and expanding the business:** Since the initial processes of setting up an online store are taken care of, you can jump straight to expanding and growing the business.

- **Investment opportunity:** Online businesses can be an important digital asset that offers a return on investment.

- **Taking over employees:** Buying an online business for sale can involve employees of the business who understand the way the business works and what they need to do to meet their job roles.

- **Right to assets:** Purchasing an online business for sale can provide you with the legal rights to assets such as patents and copyrights that the business might own.

The cons of purchasing an online business for sale

- **Upfront investment:** Based on the risk-tolerance, purchasing an online business for sale might not be the best decision for you.

- **Looking for the correct business:** To find the right online business for sale can be a time-consuming process and can involve a lot of searching, investigation, and back & forth between you and the seller.

- **Assessing the business:** Because it's an online business for sale, it can be hard to determine the business because you can't see everything in person.

- **You don't have total control over the business:** While acquiring an online business for sale can be a great asset, it can also imply that you own the business and all its assets plus capital whether you like it or not, especially when the business doesn't turn out to be everything you thought it would be.

Who can purchase an online business for sale?

Purchasing an online business for sale may be a great solution for some entrepreneurs, and not the best way for others. The same way it takes a specific entrepreneur to develop a business from scratch and work through the long hours of hustling and grinding the business creation process, the same can be considered for an entrepreneur who is ready to step into a developing and profitable online business.

Three methods to purchase an established online business

Big brands have a large retail-environment advantage over other companies because of their distribution. Now, everything is on a level playing field. You don't need to have a national brand to create a million-dollar online business.

A great product, combined with the right advertisement platform and sound audience-targeting, can quickly generate profitability for a no-name brand in a short time.

Not every entrepreneur will prefer to start a business from square one. Instead, some like to buy an established website.

We recommend these 2 platforms:

www.flippa.com

www.empireflippers.com

Chapter 9: Create a Forum

With the rise of social network discussion groups such as Facebook Groups, it appears that online forum and communities tend to become less active.

Another reason is because of the introduction of a software called "Xrumer", commonly used by Spammers to post thousands of messages in forums in just minutes, making it difficult for administrators to maintain the forum.

But, online communities have been around for a long period of time. There are different reasons why forums are still active and a preferred venue by people.

How to launch a forum?

In this chapter, you will learn how to begin and market a discussion forum.

A forum should act as a supplement to your website and not be a standalone site. Therefore, if you already own a website, add a forum. It is difficult to begin only with a discussion forum because at the start, there are no members to take part in the discussions and spread the word about your community.

Reasons to start a forum

Some of the reasons why discussion forums are still important:

- The forum can be designed to serve any long-term topic
- The level of information present can increase quickly

- Subjects are archived, letting new-generation subscribers benefit from old topics
- You can build an active members base
- An easy way to rapidly respond to reader questions or to many readers at one time
- You receive fresh content created by your members

Various disadvantages of adding a forum to your site

- You need some good traffic or your forum will remain silent without any posts
- You need to work hard and create a moderate number of posts to ensure the forum remains alive
- If your forum becomes less popular, your traffic can rise during periods of hot topic discussions and use more site bandwidth

How can you then make it work for today's tough competition – in particular, with the increase of social networks and other friendly communities?

You must be driven by passion and not money

It's important to have a financial plan created, but it should never be your project's main motivator. In fact, many managers of forums make money today because of the deep, admirable love they experience for the community's subject topic. That takes us to the next point –

Know how communities operate

Do you currently visit each website you were once a loyal fan of? Chances are, you have gone past this point, even if the said website is still powerful.

It's part of human nature to go through different cycles in life. This implies that winning a given number of subscribers can never be enough. By the time you double or triple that amount, most of the previous users will have moved to other areas.

Consider a forum for quitting smoking or overcoming a divorce. The members will remain active for a year or even more than a year, but when the problem is solved, they will proceed on with their life.

Despite this, there will be certain members that will remain loyal because they have friends there who will assist them to get over their problems. Additionally, there will be new members that will register every day because they want to be assisted with their problems.

This brings us to the next point.

Be ready to work hard and tirelessly

Without sugarcoating, it is difficult to control a forum. People who register to a relatively empty forum are unlikely to begin a conversation. But how can you get the ball rolling if you want people to interact?

The best thing is to hit the ground running by:

Inviting people to take part: You may have a lot of connections or people that you may know. Simply check your Facebook profile, or politely request your friends to help you out. Provide an incentive if you want.

Hire someone or ask for a volunteer: If you have little money, sites such as Craigslist will let you post free gig listings.

Remain active: Getting the forum active also implies being there to reply to questions and begin new topics every day. Set aside an hour or two, and scan through your forum and respond to questions from members, delete spam and post exciting content, or even ask questions that will allow your members to participate.

Provide some incentives and plan contents: When you have few members, it is important to motivate them to sign up and create posts. You will get good results by providing incentives for signing up.

Now, let's look at critical things that will help you set up a forum

Select a niche topic

A focused forum will generate more money in the long term. While you may have fewer signups, increasing the level of interaction in your forum may be a good idea, but profit depends on quality instead of quantity.

Keep in mind that you should select a niche that you know much about, or a topic that you are passionate about. It can be funny if you receive questions from your members and you don't know how to respond to. Plus, with something that you are not passionate about, you will slowly become less active in, which will chase people away.

Luckily, researching for a niche has become easier with the launch of different online communities and software. You can check out some of these online communities to get ideas of your niche:

- **Reddit:** Scan through thousands of sub-reddits and find out the number of years they have been existing, how many subscribers they have, and pay attention to the level of attention garnered. You will realize that each subject has a loyal member, but you must not forget the financial viability of your selected niche.

- **YahooAnswers and Quora:** Scan through new, trending, and all-time popular questions on the above sites. Find out what the type of questions that pop up often are. What do you think you can provide your members if you were to begin a forum based on the said topic?

- **Google Trends**: Set up email alerts involving your selected topic on Google Trends. You can turn any trend into a forum topic by asking questions about it. This is a hot cake. You can apply Google Alerts to set up notices for your specific niche.

- **Browse the same forums elsewhere:** What subjects do they cover? What are they missing? How are the members treated there? Can you table something new, or even improve on existing methods? You should not attempt to emulate an existing forum unless you have more money and time to overtake it. Instead, it will be a lost battle from the start. Ensure that your forum has something unique that will make visitors opt to spend time there.

Select a domain name

A domain name represents your address on the internet. It is not expensive to sign up for a domain name. A different path is to purchase an already registered domain. You can do this if:

- Most popular names have been taken by domain brokers.
- Old domains have the SEO power
- Old domains have a great chunk of traffic that will assist you to grow your community faster.

Select a hosting company

The first thing you want to do is to determine your current web-hosting company and look at your other options. If you are happy with your current web hosting company and would not like to move, you can decide to use some monitoring tools to ensure your hosting is the best.

The best cost when you start a forum is to include VPS and when your forum begins to trend, then you have to migrate to a dedicated server.

Chapter 10: Create a Podcast

Podcasting is a great method to express your thoughts and opinions and meet listeners from all over the world. You simply need to look for a good podcasting microphone, some tracking headphones, a user-friendly recording and editing software to clean your podcasts with, and you're ready to begin a podcast. Regardless of how easy it might sound, you will still need to dedicate effort towards it. Ensure that you generate great content that will involve your audience and make them come back for more. If you play your cards correctly, you'll even manage to make some cash with your podcasts.

Now, how can you convert podcasting into a lucrative career? This section will outline some of the more popular methods that podcasters use to generate money from their content. If you are just getting started, you will possibly want to begin with one strategy and work your way to achieving many different strategies interchangeably.

Products and services

Before you start to look for external help, you can begin by instructing yourself about potential customers. Do you run your own online business? Or better yet, did you begin podcasting mainly to market your podcasts? If your business is critical to your audience, then you can possibly think of methods to boost the returns of your earnings.

One strategy is to provide exclusive discounts to your audience. Don't be scared to offer your service, as the podcasting medium can assist you to gain the trust of your listeners. You can build your own merchandise once you have a good following – this can include baseball caps, shirts, mugs, and other products that might be relevant to your podcast niche.

Another way to market your services is by displaying your professional opinions on specific topics linked to your skills. For instance, if you work in the digital marketing field, it can be a great idea to handle information episodes that will let you showcase your marketing skills. This can be an easy way to attract clients.

Advertisement and sponsorships

Probably the trendiest method to generate money in the podcast sector is to search for sponsorships. There are a few podcast ad networks that can assist you to get advertisers, but you will probably require a monthly listener average count of at least 5-10k to manage to work with them. Another method is to do it yourself. Reach out to firms and request if they can sponsor you. Remember that audiences are easily turned off by insincerity, so make it a point to engage with brands that you believe in.

Most popular podcasts generate dollars at the end of every month via sponsorship using the cost-per-impression program. For example, you can make around $18 per 1,000 downloads per episode using a 15-second ad in the pre-roll slot.

Networking

Similar to building a business, building a relationship with the podcasting community can be vital to your success. After all, most deals are closed through connections with people from different industries. Meeting people will let you fulfill your potential sponsors.

Besides allowing you to uncover different monetary opportunities, creating your network can allow you to expand your audience via guest spots and engaging with other podcasters.

Podcasters receive money through donations and crowdfunding

Many podcasters use their own funds to run their podcasts, while a certain number turn to their listeners to help them.

Podcasters can direct listeners to GoFundMe campaigns or even allow donations to be paid to them directly by other methods.

Don't be scared to ask for help from your audience. If you have a lot of listeners and have engaged with them several times, you can count on it that many of them would be ready to give you donations to aid you and your podcast. Crowdfunding is a great strategy for entertainment-focused podcasts.

You can let people pledge to you via Patreon, whose subscription content service makes it easy to deliver extra content based on the amount of cash a listener or member can pay you to support. If you intend to support a charity, your podcast can be a great way for obtaining donations.

Premium content

Through Patreon, you can provide premium content that you know your audience will want to listen to. Unique examples of premium content are: Special interviews, ad-free series, and other novel content that can accept a few dollars per month.

You will realize that some podcasters provide live and video version of their audio podcasts and additional bonuses when a listener buys an annual subscription. It can be anything you can think of, as long as it fascinates your listeners and you make what they pay for count.

Hosting events

Don't forget how you build relationships via podcasts? You can take advantage of those relationships and combine them with an online digital conference where you bring in experts and celebrities to talk about a given subject.

By working together with prominent personalities, you can incorporate into their market and acquire more listeners. In exchange, your new listeners can pay to subscribe to the virtual summit and join your email list.

Books and audiobooks

This method may not work for everybody, but it can be a powerful income-generating option for those that are authors already. Utilize the opportunity to involve your podcast audience to increase the sale of your books. Plus, invite reviewers to select your material. You can still be a guest on other podcasts to market your book.

But you if you aren't an author, it doesn't mean that you cannot create an audiobook from your quality podcast content. Feel free to develop a new product as a means to catch up on and learn from the insights of your content.

In conclusion, there is more than one way to generate money from a podcast. As podcasts continue to take over the market, more and more people are taking advantage of it and creating new shows, in a move to leverage themselves as industry professionals, connect with more influencers, create personal brands, and increase exposure for their businesses.

In line with that reasoning, many people are currently using the podcast as an additional revenue mechanism for their businesses and for themselves as individuals.

So if you are interested in generating more money from podcasting, don't wait – jump in head-first and grab that opportunity.

Chapter 11: Credit Card Rewards and Cashbacks

There are many reasons why you need to think through and start using your credit card – not only for normal purchases, but for all your purchases. Here is how you can make some passive income from credit card rewards and cashbacks.

1. **Sign-up bonuses**

If your credit score is high, you will automatically qualify for a sign-up bonus of around $250 or more when you use the best credit card offers. For example, Capital One Venture Rewards Credit Card provides a bonus of around 50,000 miles after spending $3,000 in the first three months, which when converted, amounts to $500.

Certain cards offer redeemable miles, points, or plain cash just for signing up. These sign-up bonuses are like free cash.

The amount of bonus will change depending on the type of credit card you select, and normally, the ones with the best sign-up bonuses have the highest annual fees.

In most cases, these cards have a reward program.

2. **Rewards**

Most credit cards have a points system that will allow you to make some money when you apply for your card. Credit card companies provide promotions where purchases in specific sections such as restaurants generate more rewards than normal. These rewards can be redeemed for gift cards in the credit company's rewards catalog.

Another prominent alternative is the mileage reward cards, where you receive rewards for traveling. These usually come with good sign-up bonuses, and the rewards you redeem can reduce the cost of your trip. In addition, most of these cards provide perks for traveling.

3. **Cashback**

You can get cards that provide cashback rewards, thus, you need to spend money so that you will receive a check in the mail or money off your Amazon purchases. Cashback credit cards are increasing in number because of their simplicity – you don't need to fear the points or exchange rates.

Cashback credit rewards were first promoted in the USA by Discover Magazine. Nowadays, credit cards provide 2-3 percent and even 6 percent cashback for selected purchases.

4. **Convenience and safety**

Credit cards are accepted everywhere, and there are many situations where you cannot use your debit card – for instance, when you rent a car. Car rental companies like customers who pay for services via credit cards because it's easier to charge customers for any damages to the car. It is possible to rent a car and pay for it using a debit card, but the rental car company may then hold hundreds of dollars as security.

Additionally, the use of credit card for things such as car rentals and travel can offer you an additional layer of security in case something important happens.

Ways to optimize

The best method to optimize the rewards you get is to direct each purchase on a card. If you have a choice to pay using cash, check or pay using a card, some of the places you can consider to increase your returns include:

- Work/travel costs

- Purchases for rental properties

- Charitable contributions

- Gift cards. In some instances, you can purchase gift cards at a grocery store, and since a card provides 5% cashback at grocery stores, you can receive 5% on gift cards bought there. This has the ability to convert any purchase at a restaurant, department store, or home improvement store into a 5% cash back opportunity.

- Extra bonuses. Some groceries will provide bonus rewards depending on the purchases done at the store. The more you purchase, the more you can earn. Typically, purchasing gift cards will focus on purchases done at the store and thus boost rewards to a new level. Some stores still provide an additional bonus credit for gift card purchases.

Caveats

Using credit cards to generate money only works when you adhere to strict guidelines such as:

- You can't spend more than you earn just because you have a credit card. There is more research that indicates people spend more when they use a credit card. This doesn't imply that all people spend more when they use a credit card, just that you may have to guard against it.

- You can't keep balance on your credit card. You need to pay it off each month, so you need to take note of it,

- You can't pay the fees linked with your card. An annual fee may cost you, and as long as what you get out of the card is more than the annual fee, then keep the card.

Some people are scared that opening a new credit card account may reduce their credit scores and possibly cost them more than they may earn in rewards. When done correctly, especially by opening new cards without closing older ones, it seems like adding a new card now and then has a low impact on your credit score.

Our favorite:

www.ebates.com

Chapter 12: Getting a High Yield Savings Account

For most people, opening a standard savings account is the first step to help them control their personal finances. But aside from the safety and reliability of the basic accounts, they are not lucrative. The rate of interest they provide is so scant that, once inflation and fees are considered, you may lose money on the account over time.

Consider opening a high-yield savings account - also referred to as high-interest savings account - to supplement a standard account. As the name goes, this is a deposit account that will pay a higher interest rate and a higher annual percentage yield than a traditional deposit savings account.

Despite paying more, high-yield accounts share the same reassuring security – same as the other cousins. The Federal Deposit Insurance Corporation (FDIC) protects the balance of accounts in the National Credit Union Share Insurance Fund.

To start the procedure of acquiring a high-yield account, request the staffers at your bank or credit union if they can provide you with an account with a bigger interest rate than your current one. If they fail to do so, you can decide to shop for a high-yield account at other organizations.

What to search for

Even if your current bank provides a high yield choice, it could be wise to compare what is available elsewhere. The differences in interest fees and rates can add up with time, especially with the large balance you might have to maintain in a high-yield savings account.

Below are things to analyze and compare high-yield accounts:

- **The required initial deposit.** This is the amount of money needed to open the account.

- **Rate of interest.** The amount of interest you will make on your balance. Will the rate be temporary?

- **Earnings from compounding.** The rate of interest is the main driver of a savings account, but the way in which the interest is compounded and computed impacts the yields. There are different compounding procedures – including daily, monthly, semi-annually, annually, and quarterly. The more times the interest is compounded, the higher the yields. The account's annual percentage yield (APY) considers compounding into account, reflecting both the interest rate and the frequency with which the interest is applied.

- **Links to other Banks.** Does the account permit you to develop links between the funds in the above account and the one you hold in other bank accounts? This link will let you easily transfer money in and out of the account.

- **Application and maintenance fees.** How much does the bank or credit union charge to open the new account?

- **Required extra accounts.** Sometimes, banks may ask you to provide an additional account like a checking account so as to open the savings account. Sometimes, you can open those extra accounts so that you receive the bank's best high-yield interest rate. You might need to examine whether the utility and additional costs of the supplementary accounts can make the high-yield account insignificant.

- **The number of transactions.** This is critical when you take into consideration an account with a bank. How can you manage to deposit into the account: By wire, mail or bank transfer? Can you do it using the ATMs of other banks?

- **Accessing money.** What options are present for withdrawing the funds? Can you create checks against the account?

High yield accounts and finances

A high-yield savings account should involve only a portion of your general financial portfolio. Consider how you can best use the account to complement other savings and investment accounts.

For instance, estimate the amount of cash sufficient to support liquidity via a high-yield savings account. Is that amount an estimate of the money you need to cover certain circumstances or a set dollar amount?

Next, figure out the kind of actions you need to take once you attain that financial threshold. Will you move the money out of the account and direct it to a different interest-bearing accounts or investments? You can also consider alternatives like paying down debt, beginning a college fund for children, or beginning a business.

Alternatively, consider the best way to move funds in and out of the high-yield account. For instance, some accounts will let you roll into the account the principal and interest generated on a CD without any penalty, when the CD grows.

The point is that a high-yield savings account can be a great ground for your money, providing both the security of the federal insurance and a yield that is higher than a regular account, even if it is less than you could earn from a riskier investment. But before you can open such an account, check first how it fulfills your finances as a whole. That approach can assist you to make decisions on the amount to deposit in the account and what features you may need.

Pros and Cons of a High-Interest Savings Account

There is no minimum balance needed

Without fearing the penalty fees when your funds are lower than the minimum balance needed in a saving account, directing your money into a high-interest savings accounts can be a safe way to earn passively. This is far better if you are an employee who sustains everyday life only from paycheck to paycheck. With this setup, you can make the most of your money in times of financial need and avoid fearing fulfillment of a balance needed in your account.

Much higher interest rates

Contrary to investing in money market fund accounts, you don't need to learn the trends and stay current with the news to increase your interest and compound them over time. Consider the literal meaning of a high-interest savings account – you can make high-yield savings with higher interest rates. The percentages are different based on the rates provided by the financial institution and the amount deposited.

Cons of high-interest savings account

Limited withdrawals

Unlike regular savings and checking accounts, high-interest savings account would only allow you to make a specific number of withdrawals. Some banks even tell depositors of these accounts to forget about withdrawing their money for some months or years. If you are an employee, it might be a great thing to set aside a certain percentage of your cash to this savings account and have a different account where you can withdraw money for your daily expenditures. This is to enable the bank double the amount of interest you can generate later on.

Temporary introductory rates

When you decide to open a high-interest savings account, you must consider the introductory rates provided. Understand that the above alluring rates are just temporary and once the "honeymoon" stage expires, your account will acquire interest depending on the standard rates of the bank, which are normally lower. Without any prior notice, banks have the right to change interest rates on a monthly basis. Before you invest your money in a bank that provides a high-interest savings account, do your research and identify the terms to make a decision whether or not to take the chance or pass it up.

As an employee who desires to save the best for your future, you might enjoy the fruits of saving in a high-savings interest account. The main thing is to uphold discipline, and avoid withdrawing money into this account and allow the interest to increase with time. If you aren't sure if you can maintain this, you can organize with your employer to set aside a certain percentage of your monthly income into this account. This way, you can optimize the probability of earning more money via interest while saving yourself the hassle of handling other complex investments.

Chapter 13: Hedge Forex for Swap Gains

"Currency risk" refers to the financial risk that emerges from possible changes in the exchange rate of a particular currency with reference to another one.

This doesn't only affect the ones trading in the foreign exchange market. But intense currency movements can destroy the profits of a portfolio with deep international exposure, or crush the returns of a prosperous international business venture.

The companies that run business across borders are exposed to currency risk when income received abroad is converted into the money of the domestic country, and when payables are transformed from the domestic currency to the foreign currency.

The currency swap industry is one method to hedge that risk. Apart from hedging against risk exposure related to exchange rate changes, currency swaps also acknowledge the receipt of foreign monies and attain better lending rates.

How currency swaps operate

A "currency swap" describes a financial instrument that facilitates the exchange of interest in one currency for the same in a different currency.

Currency swaps include two notional principals exchanged at the start and end of the agreement. These notional principals include pre-determined dollar amounts, on which the exchanged interest payments feature. But this principle is not repaid – it is just notional. It is only applied as a basis on which to compute the interest rate payments.

Check with various brokers on their swap policies and they usually are able to provide you with a chart. Look out for those positive swap pairs that will generate a "rollover interest". You will then put an open position and start earning daily swaps!

Beware of margin calls though.

Chapter 14: Invest in Annuities

An annuity refers to an insurance product that pays income and can be used as a retirement plan. Annuities are the best choices for investors who want to earn a continuous stream of income in retirement.

While they are marketed as investments, annuities aren't investments. They are contracts. They bind you and the insurance company into a contractual agreement.

Annuities have been in existence for centuries. In Ancient Rome, people can make a single payment in return for a yearly lifetime payment. Even now, retirement planning is still a subject of interest.

Annuities became popular in USA during the time of the Great Depression. This was the time when people started to be worried about stock market volatility endangering their retirement. As of today, with the pension plans becoming less common, many retirees are depending on annuities as a substitute to income streams.

You can purchase annuity because it does something that other investments cannot do – that is, to offer guaranteed income for the rest of your life regardless of how long you live.

Beyond these basics, there are some simple annuities. Annuities and the rules under which they work can be difficult, so it may help to acknowledge that a common source of retirement income/social security is a type of annuity.

How does annuity work?

Annuity operates by transferring some of the risks to the owner. Like other forms of insurance, you pay the annuity company a premium to handle the risk. Premiums can include a single lump sum or a sequence of payments, based on the type of annuity purchased. The premium-paying interval is called the "accumulation" phase.

Unlike other forms of insurance, annuity premiums aren't paid indefinitely. Finally, you stop paying the annuity and the annuity begins to pay you. When this takes place, your contract is defined to have gone into a "payout" phase.

There's a large flexibility in the way annuity payments are taken care of. Annuities can be designed to activate payments for a fixed number of years to you, until when you and your spouse pass away, or a combination of both lifetime incomes with an assured "period certain" payout. A plan with a "period certain" annuity will pay income for life, but in case you die in a given time frame, the annuity will pay your beneficiary the notice of your payments for the contractual period you select at the time of application.

Similar to social security, annuity lifetime income streams depend on the recipient's life expectancy, with small payouts accepted over a longer period. Therefore, a longer life expectancy results in a smaller payment.

Payments can occur on a monthly basis, quarterly basis, annual basis, or even a lump sum. They can begin immediately, or be postponed for some years – even decades.

Annuities are heavily customized. Identifying an annuity to fulfill your needs waters down to two questions: First, what do you want the money to contractually do? And when do you want the contractual guarantees to begin?

An instant annuity starts paying income instantly

While it's annuitized instantly, an instant annuity doesn't begin paying income immediately. You make a single lump sum payment to the insurance company, and it starts paying you income one annuity period after buying it. This can be 30 days to one year later.

The timeframe depends on the frequency you decide to receive income payments. For example, if you select monthly payments, your first instant annuity payment will emerge one month after your purchase. Since payments start soon, instant annuities are popular among retirees.

Differed annuities offer tax-advantaged savings and lifetime income

When you have a deferred annuity, you start to receive payments in the coming years. At the same time, your premiums grow tax-deferred inside the annuity. They are normally used to supplement personal retirement accounts and employer-sponsored retirement plans because the majority of the annuities have no Internal Revenue Service (IRS)-contribution limits.

Annuity investments

Investors purchase annuities from insurance firms to make sure they have sufficient income to support them when they retire, since annuity represents a fixed-amount payment paid at constant intervals. An investor receives the payments in exchange for contributing an initial lump sum. An annuity contract can remain active for the whole life of the policyholder. As a result, they provide protection against longevity. Payouts don't necessarily increase because of inflation, but specific contracts offer inflation security.

There are different types of annuities: A deferred annuity is similar to payments deferred until a future date. In exchange for this deferral, payments in the future can be higher than instant annuities where payments begin soon after an investor purchases them for an additional lump sum. Variable annuities integrate insurance and investing, where future payouts depend on the underlying investments. These can be profits generated from index-based investments. They can still provide a specific type of protection in case a stock market profit drops below a given level.

Chapter 15: Invest in Bonds and Use Leverage to Buy

How to invest in bonds for starters

Many of us like to borrow money to use to complete a project, or when we forget our cash at home. The same way borrowing is part of our daily life, it is something to uphold by companies and municipalities. Even the federal government does the same – it provides bonds.

Bonds come in different forms: It can be municipal bonds, corporate, or government bonds. They are all the same at their core. When an entity releases a bond, it requests for a specific investment of cash. Next, it promises to pay back the investment, plus some interest.

How do bonds work?

If you buy a bond, you will loan a certain percentage of money to the bond issuer for a given time period. Then, the issuer sets the date of when to pay the regular interest until the bond is finished. But there are some exceptions – people who don't pay the interest, but buy at face value. Despite this, most bonds follow the general formula, that is: Invest some money, collect interest payments, and receive money back once it matures.

How to make money from bonds?

There are two strategies you can use to make money investing in bonds:

First, stay with the bonds until they hit the maturity period, and then enjoy the interest. The interest of the bonds is always paid twice per year.

Another method to generate money from bonds is to sell it at a higher price than the initial price. For example, you sell a bond of $5,000 at $7,000. In this scenario the $2,000 is yours.

Now let's look at the types of bonds

Here is a list of different types of bonds:

- Corporate bonds. These are bonds given by corporations to increase business-related operations. For corporate bonds, there is a higher interest than any other bond.

- Municipal bonds. Provided by the state and cities. There are two types: General obligation and revenue.

- Treasury bonds. These bonds are given by the United States. The interest you earn from these bonds is taxed at the federal level. The maturity period of treasury bonds is 10 years.

How can you make money from bonds as an investor?

Bonds are part of fixed-income securities.

Holders of bonds can earn money on bonds in two ways:

First, as interest payments is referred to as a "coupon", in the whole life of the bond.

Next, bonds change in price. This change in price depends on different factors, the most critical of which is the interest rate in the market. Certain investors try to make money from price fluctuations of bonds by making a guess where the interest rates will go.

How investors can generate money from a zero-coupon bond

An investor generates money on a zero-coupon bond by getting paid interest once it matures. The party that issues the bond doesn't pay the whole value.

The power of leverage will make you rich

It is important to apply leverage if you want to become wealthy. In fact, you need to include a huge amount of leverage. The more leverage you involve, the more you need to use. A popular notion is that leverage refers only to borrowing money – leverage is more than that.

Leverage is the ability to do a lot of things with little. Through leverage, you can cause more change rapidly. Leverage equals velocity or speed.

Leverage is using borrowed money to invest with so that you can increase returns. For instance, you can have $200 that you can invest. But instead of purchasing $200 in stocks, you choose to purchase $500 of stocks. If the stocks increase by 10%, you can earn $50 of profit instead of $20 you would have earned in the initial investment of $200.

Investing with leverage isn't gambling

It is important to know that investing isn't gambling. Although gambling depends on the probability of specific events taking place, investing is different. As a result, you should be preoccupied with the value of something instead of guessing whether the price will increase or decrease.

With this, there is only one reason of applying leverage: To boost your returns on investments. In one way, you can consider it as "conservative-aggressive" investing. You only invest when there is a big-value price difference – and you invest heavily into those chances.

How to smartly use leverage

The smartest and best investors use leverage successfully. To do the same, you must first use leverage selectively. It is not a good thing to overdo it with borrowing money. Leverage is a double-edged sword, and displaying your risks in an oversized and constant way can affect you. Instead, you should only apply leverage on a chosen few opportunities for which you have the largest knowledge.

Next, the average investor should apply different leverage devices based on the opportunities available. For instance, by trading on a margin or with Contract for Differences (CFDs), it is much better for longer-term trades that are focused at gradual closing of the value-price gap.

It can also be attractive to purchase dividend-type securities on a margin, as long as you have the confidence in the underlying issuer's strength. Alternatively, applying options can be a great way to boost your returns if you have a high conviction on specific events taking place in the short term.

Finally, it is better to begin to use leverage when you are young. There are various reasons why leverage is perfect for people in the 20s rather than for people who are about to retire. First, young people have low capital, and hence aren't exposed to many risks in the stock market. Besides that, young people should possess a higher risk tolerance than their older counterparts. Losing some hundred to thousand dollars can affect, but it won't destroy your life. But losing a big percentage of your retirement portfolio can.

Lastly, investors should be aware of what they purchase. As long as you invest, using leverage can be a productive mechanism.

Chapter 16: How to Invest in Dividend Stocks

Are you looking for an investment that generates regular income? Dividend stocks can be a great choice.

Dividend stocks spread a specific size of the company's earnings to investors on a constant basis. Most American dividend stocks pay investors a specific amount every quarter, and the top ones increases the payouts over time. Therefore, investors can create an annuity-like cash stream. Investors can decide to reinvest dividends.

Dividend stocks appear to be less volatile than growth stocks. Therefore, they assist in diversifying one's general portfolio and eliminate risk.

How to purchase dividends

You will learn two methods to invest in dividend stocks: Through buying individual dividend stocks, and exchange-traded funds (ETFs) that hold the stocks. Let's begin with dividend ETFs because they are the simplest.

Investing in dividend stocks via ETFs

Like what happens in the world of ETFs, dividend ETFs provides a simple and straightforward solution to receiving exposure to a particular investing niche – in the following case, stocks that pay a frequent dividend.

A dividend ETF normally involves dozens, if not hundreds, of dividend stocks. That immediately offers you diversification, which implies greater safety for your payout. Even when a few of the fund's stocks reduce their dividends, the effect will be less on the fund's entire dividend. A safe payout should be your top selection in purchasing any dividend-paying investment.

Below is how to purchase a dividend stock ETF

1. **Select a broadly diversified dividend ETF.**

You can basically find dividend ETFs by searching for it on your broker's website.

Perhaps the safest option is a low-cost fund that selects dividend stocks form the S&P 500 stock index. That provides a broadly defined package of America's top companies. You may want to limit your search to commission-free choices, so you don't pay a commission every time you sell the ETF.

2. **Analyze the ETF.**

Ensure the ETF is invested in stocks, and not bonds. You may also want to confirm the following:

- The dividend yield: This is the amount a company pays out in dividends every year, relative to its price share, and is often displayed as a percentage. In general, higher is preferable, although anything above 3.5% should be checked closely to examine the safety of the investment.

- 5-year returns: Overall, higher is better.

- Expense ratio: This is the ETF's annual fee, paid out of your investment in the fund. Search for an expense ratio that is below 0.5%, but lower is preferred.

- The size of the stock: The dividend ETFs can be invested in companies with massive, medium or small capitalization. Large caps are the safest, while small caps are the riskiest.

3. Purchase the ETF

You can purchase the ETFs just like the way you do with a stock. A nice approach is to purchase them often, so as to take advantage of dollar-cost averaging.

Why you need to purchase an ETF: The biggest problem for individual investors is that you can purchase only one ETF and don't have to monitor dozens of companies, which is something you wish to avoid doing if you purchase dividend stocks yourself. Purchase your dividend ETF and then add money to it often.

Investing in REIT

You can also earn passive income by investing in a real estate investment trust (REIT) that owns, manages, and maintains investment properties. Investing in a publicly traded REIT is an easy option to place your cash into a portfolio of real estate investments the same way you may invest in a mutual fund.

What is an REIT?

Most REITs work in a manner that's straightforward and easy to follow through. They buy a property and then rent or lease that property to businesses or residents to earn income. The income is then paid out to investors in the form of dividends.

When you invest in a REIT, you invest in a real estate portfolio controlled and planned by a company. A REIT is needed to pay out at least 90% of its taxable income to shareholders – though it can do whatever it does to attain the 100% mark.

REITs generally own about $3 trillion worth of real estate in the United States.

Steps to purchase a REIT

1. Know the types of REITS

The first step to investing in real estate, or investing in REITs, is to know that there are different types to select from. Some of the most popular REITs you will encounter include:

Equity REITs

An equity REIT is the most popular type of REIT and works by buying properties and renting them to third parties. The REIT is responsible for managing these properties. If you see the term "REIT" listed anywhere, the writer will essentially describe an equity REIT unless specified otherwise.

Mortgage REITs

The mortgage REITs work by releasing funds for mortgages to income-generating properties. Next, they collect payout dividends starting from the interest these mortgages create.

Non Public-listed REITs

These are registered with the SEC, but aren't publicly traded.

Private REITs

These have not been listed on public exchanges and are exempt from SEC registration. You will need to have special access to invest in the following type of REIT.

2. Analyze risks related to investing in REITS

Though investing in REITs is said to be a stable and safe investment, it is still vital for prospective investors to know the specific risks related to REITs:

More expense ratios

Since the properties associated with REITs need to be actively controlled, expense ratios for REITs seem to be higher than other types of equities. A high expense ratio, integrated with a REIT that isn't generating expense-justifying dividends, can be a recipe for lost money.

Legal liabilities

There are multiple laws for managing the rights of the renter, property leases and titles. Legal disputes that involve unpaid dues and landlord responsibilities can be long, and the bills for the following disputes are usually placed on the shoulders of the REIT investors in terms of reduced dividends.

Risks in liquidity

The liquidity status of REITs is lower than bonds because they need high minimum investments. Investors wanting to sell their REITs may have challenges in finding buyers.

3. **Select a brokerage firm**

REITs are traded publicly, so you can decide to invest in them in the same way as stocks and bonds. The first step to make a REIT is to identify a broker if you don't open an account. If you want to invest in a non-publicly traded REIT, then you will need to get in touch with a broker with permission for that REIT.

Still, you can invest in REITs via publicly-traded ETFs.

4. **Place an order**

Once you choose a REIT that you are interested in buying, the process of making an order to purchase will resemble your platform's process for purchasing a stock or bond.

Sign onto your account and switch to your broker's page to purchase stocks and funds. Search the name of the REIT or the ticker of the

REIT, enter the order type you would like and the number of shares you would like to buy. Re-check the information you have typed so that it is correct, and place your order.

Although there are genuine and profitable private REITs, you should be concerned about anyone trying to sell shares of a REIT that isn't registered with the SEC.

You can look at the registration status of a REIT plus its annual and quarterly reports by looking for it using the SEC's EDGAR filing system. Keep in mind too, that because the REIT pays out most of its taxable income to shareholders, you are accountable for reporting and paying taxes on your received dividends.

Chapter 17: Invest in Tax Liens

The rise in the volatility of the stock market mixed with historically low interest rates has led to many investors looking for alternative means to provide a decent rate of return. One investment method that is always overlooked is property tax liens.

Every homeowner understands the "joy" of paying property taxes. Unfortunately, with so many challenges in life, it has become difficult for people to clear their bills.

When a homeowner is unable to pay taxes for his or her property, a lien is put on their house and the tax lien certificate is auctioned off to investors.

Anyone can take part in a tax lien auction and they are very popular with small investors. Also, tax liens can also be bought for as low as $100, making it accessible even for those people with the least capital.

The unique opportunity that a tax lien creates offers investors with good rates of return. Property liens also carry significant risks – thus, novice buyers must know the rules and possible pitfalls that emerge with investing in the following asset.

Property tax liens are available at the municipality, letting the lien owner gather payments with interest on the property.

How can you then invest in tax liens?

When a lien is released, a tax lien certificate is generated by the municipality that represents the amount owed on the property, including any interest and penalties due. The certificates are auctioned off and given to the highest bidder. For as little as a few hundred dollars, you can purchase tax liens, but most cost more than this.

The auctions can be held in a physical place, and investors may bid down on the rate of interest that they will pay for it. The investor who is ready to accept the lowest rate of interest wins the lien. You should note that buyers always enter into bidding conflict over a certain property, which will reduce the rate of return that is acquired by the winning buyer.

Although the national foreclosure rate on properties with tax liens is just about 4%, buyers have to be careful on the cost of repairs and other unknown factors that they need to pay if they assume property ownership. Those who own these properties may have to deal with unattractive tasks, such as kicking out the current occupants, which may require help from an attorney.

Those interested in buying a tax lien can begin by choosing the type of property they would like to hold a line. This can be a residential, commercial, or undeveloped land with improvements. They can then get in touch with their city treasurer to identify when, where and how the next auction will be conducted. The office of the treasurer can inform the investor where to find a list of property liens that have been scheduled to be auctioned, plus the regulations on how the sale will be done. These rules will define any pre-registration requirements, approved payment methods, and other pertinent details.

Buyers should also perform due diligence on properties available because sometimes, the current value of the property can be less than the amount of the lien. According to the NTLA, one should divide the face amount of the delinquent tax lien by the market value of the property. If the ratio is more than 4%, prospective buyers should steer clear of that property. In addition, there could be other liens on the property that can affect the bidder from owning it.

Each piece of real estate in a particular county with a tax lien is allocated a number within its respective parcel. Buyers can search for these liens using a number to obtain information about them from the county, which can be online. For every number, the county has the property address, the assessed value of the property, the name of the owner, legal description, and a breakdown of the status of the property and any structures assigned on the premises.

How to make returns from a lien?

Individuals who buy property tax liens need to instantly pay the amount of the lien in full back to the issuing municipality. In all but two states, the tax lien issuer gathers the principal, interest, and any penalties to pay the lien certificate holder and gather the lien certificate if it's absent in file. The owner of the property must repay the investor the whole amount of the lien including the interest, which can range between 5%-36%, but it is normally between 10%-12%. When an investor pays a premium for the lien, this can be added to the amount that is repaid in certain cases.

The repayment plan lasts from six months to three years. In some cases, the owner may fail to pay the lien by the deadline. In such a case, the investor has permission to foreclose on the property just as the municipality has, although this is a rare case.

Challenges of investing in property tax liens

While tax liens can generate significant rates of interest, investors must do their research before making the final decision. Tax liens are not good for novice investors, or those with little knowledge of real estate.

Investors must be familiar with the initial property in which the lien is placed, to make sure they can gather the money from the owner. A dilapidated property assigned in the heart of a slum neighborhood is perhaps not a great purchase, no matter the rate of interest promised, because the owner of the property can fail to pay the tax owed. Properties that have been subjected to environmental damage are also unattractive.

Owners of a lien must know their duties after they get their certificates. They must alert the property owner in writing of their purchase within a specific amount of time, and then they must send a second letter of notification to them near the end of the redemption time if the payment hasn't been made in full by the deadline.

Tax liens are not stable instruments. Most of them have a date of expiration after the end of their redemption period. If the lien expires, the lien holder cannot collect any unpaid balance. If the property goes into foreclosure, the lien holder can discover other liens on the property, which can make it hard to attain the title deed.

We also recommend this book on tax liens:

Real Estate Investing Through Tax Liens & Deeds
By me, Phil C. Senior

Chapter 18: Investing in Cheap Cars for UBER Rental

We know what you're thinking:

"I want my car! Why should I rent it out for a little extra cash?"

But read on to find out.

How much do you need your car?

How often do you even use your car?

Do you use it 24/7?

If not, then you could be earning a good amount of cash with your car.

Consider all the hours your car stays outside every day.

That is an unused opportunity.

Every second your car goes unused, is a second you could use to make money. But you are perhaps not making a single dollar, because you are not renting out your car when it sits outside. Nowadays, fewer people are using cars than before. Many people are working from home on their computers. They are not spending countless hours chasing traffic daily. They are not spending a fortune on gas every month. And this is a good thing.

But what happens to that car that they initially used to depend on to transport them to their workstation?

It only sits there… and they start to think about things at random. For example:

- Can I rent my car to Uber?
- Can I rent my car to someone?
- You can also say, "I want to rent my car."

There is no point in owning a car which you don't use. Now, people who find themselves in this situation sell their car.

That makes sense: Get some thousand dollars, spend it in several months. Purchase groceries. Or even venture to bring yourself on a vacation or purchase some new clothes.

But what if someone told you that there was another method of generating continuous passive income using your car?

What if you didn't just get paid a thousand bucks once, but every single month?

Yes, this is really possible, and you are going to see how, shortly.

You know the power of passive income, and this is another great way to earn money without breaking a sweat.

Implement this whole plan, and you will generate passive income with virtually no effort.

1% of the population knows that the real secret to wealth is via passive income.

It is time for you to think of implementing the program.

Sure, you won't become rich by renting out your Honda Accord.

But still, it is a great source of income – one that requires the least work.

Integrate this with other passive income streams, and soon you will be earning a six-figure salary.

Before you get started, it is important to underline a few things:

Renting out your car isn't a good idea if you've fallen in love with your car. Don't rent out your prized Gran Torino. If you don't feel comfortable letting other people use your car, then don't.

It is that simple.

If you are comfortable with other people touching your car, then you should consider renting out your car.

Who can you rent your car?

This is the most important question.

Don't be scared; you are not going to rent your car to strangers on the street.

Instead, you will be using a professional contract. With this plan, you will be working with professional businesses and organizations. There are different organizations to select from. The most obvious is Uber, and this a popular lift-service having businesses all over the world.

Another option is Ola.

Turo is also a great company working in North America.

There are many other options that are not mentioned here.

Uber or Ola

You can decide to rent out your car to both of these companies using the same procedure.

When you rent your car to Uber, you are basically hiring a driver to work on your behalf. The driver then pays you a percentage of what he or she earns.

Both Uber and Ola have the whole systems in place that makes renting out a car easy and simple. You will have everything completed in a couple of days.

This is a really good choice because most Uber drivers work at night.

Even if you are going to use your car during the day, you are perhaps not using it all night. While your car is sitting out there in the cold night, you can as well let it generate some dollars for you.

An Uber driver will come to take your car, make some money, and then bring it back for you to leave for work in the morning.

You will make some good passive income while sleeping.

Travel agencies

In certain countries, you may have the chance to rent your car to travel agencies on a daily basis. However, this one will demand some strong networking skills on your side. It will also be easier if you have a luxury car. Although this option may provide less freedom than Uber, you can still include in your contract how often you want the car per week and on which days in particular.

With the correct negotiation skills, this can be a profitable choice.

Why contracts are important

Renting out your car doesn't have to be that risky.

It is easy to ensure that your expenses are taken care of with the right contract. Based on who you are working with, the contract can differ. All in all, a contract plays the same function no matter what.

In your contract, you can include all the worries you have.

Companies such as Uber or Ola have their own contract that you must sign. Read the contract carefully, and ensure everything is covered. Things like insurance and damages are very important. But

Uber's contract should cover everything. It should protect both parties, and they cannot scam you with the contract.

Contracts are critical when you are working with smaller agencies and organizations. In this situation, you will both build your unique contract, so there is more freedom. This also implies that there's more room for mistakes, so you must be careful.

When working with these companies, you may also want to look at their business license and other relevant documents. You probably need to verify that they are legitimate.

At the end of the day, all contracts eliminate worry about your car. With the correct documentation in place, there's no danger for financial loss on your side.

More concerns

There are a few other worries that you need to take note of if you decide to rent out your car.

Keep a close eye on these factors, and you should not worry about a single thing while your contract is generating money on your behalf.

Maintain your car in great condition

Expensive cars cost more to rent out. So if you want to earn more money, you must keep your car in top condition.

Your car should go through regular maintenance, but it's more important when you rent it out to other people. Can you imagine how much it will cost if your car breaks down when someone is trying to avoid getting late?

No question that they wouldn't want to rent from you again in the future.

The appearance of your car is also important. A quick decent car can work miracles, and instantly, your average car will appear luxurious.

Little details make a big difference – add a scent diffuser to make the car smell well. Polish the interior of the car. It all sparks the monetary worth of your car. You can even decide to apply a fresh coat of paint. While it may demand some effort, it might increase your income in the long run.

Identify expired documents

It's also important to ensure that your car's documents are up-to-date. Confirm that your insurance papers are up-to-date. If you accidentally let your documents expire, you might face big problems, based on the type of company using your car.

You don't want to consider what can happen if your car is involved in a serious accident, and the insurance policy isn't up to code.

Other factors like proof of registration are crucial. In general, you should keep your relevant documents in your car all the time.

Security deposit

If you choose to work with a smaller company, you may want to choose to have a security deposit before you hand over your vehicle.

You cannot know what may happen. Even when you have a strong contract in place, you must be ready for the unknown.

If your car is totaled by some strange occurrences, and you don't have a contract to cover it, you still have a security deposit as a small safety net.

You can still elaborate in your contract when the security deposit becomes forfeited. For instance, a driver may cause a total mess in the car. You can then apply the security deposit and use it for cleaning costs.

Such small things make a security deposit valuable in the long run.

How much can you make?

If you consider this a serious passive income venture, there is a serious question left to answer:

How much can you generate?

The response to this question can make or break the deal.

If you are only making a few dollars per month, is it really worth?

On the flipside, making just a few thousand dollars per year can be really good.

It depends on the type of companies you are working with.

For Uber, they provide the least amount of income with this strategy. The reason is that you are sharing your income with many other people. The driver takes his or her share, and so does the company itself. At the end of the day, you are only going to make a few extra bucks each night.

But still, some people can be okay with just a small extra income. The argument still holds: If your car is sitting idle in your driveway, it is way better for it to earn you some income... Right?

Also, you need to think about the current state of Uber. Uber drivers around the world go on strike often, stating that it's hard to make a substantial income. If they aren't making enough profit, then you will not cash in a lot once you rent out your car to Uber.

Uber has the tendency to take a bigger share of the money, regardless of whether you are driving or someone who is renting out a car.

At the end of the day, this passive income strategy has a huge potential. It is a great thing to work with a reputable company because they will have contracts and the whole system structured.

If you are looking to add more passive income streams to your list, this could be a great option.

Chapter 19: Make a Real World Service and Outsource the Work

In the business sector, big companies at some point dominated the side of outsourcing that was not accessible to smaller businesses.

The advantages of outsourcing are endless, but it always scales down to saving your time and money, and making more money by using your time wisely.

Many companies that are in the start-up phase benefit the most and the largest benefit is leveraging on time. Time is the biggest asset in any business – not money. The most frequent things that companies outsource are back-end tasks like funnel design, payroll processing, customer support, and an in-house team.

There are several things that you need to be aware of before you outsource any project or task: What is your goal in outsourcing, and how may your company benefit? What is it that you want completed by outsourcing? How much time and money are you saving?

Here's what you need to do to improve your business efficiency:

Areas where outsourcing can benefit your business

Lowered costs

This can be the main reason why a startup can get ahead faster – by saving money. And many huge corporations outsource on a large scale to scale down on manufacturing costs. According to research, a company can save about 60% on operational costs with an outsourced party.

Customer service

When it comes to marketing, customer service is the biggest asset to improve on. Hiring a few people to handle customer support is a great business. Entrepreneurs have gained a lot from outsourcing repeated tasks, giving them more time and chances to expand their business.

Reduced risk

Each business can run smoothly, and can be able to take on more than one task or build campaigns. Saving time can open new channels to other places in your market. Automation is also crucial in this area, and some of the internet tasks using assistance from experienced individuals can improve the operation.

Increased efficiency and productivity

It's the joy of every person in a company when things run smoothly. This saves time and opens doors to other areas in your life. Automation also assists in this area, and some of the internet tasks using assistance from experienced people makes the operation productive, making more money.

Use your time wisely

Time is the most sought thing after asset in any business. The second is money. So in business, you are going to develop a system and a team to help you leverage your time. In a brick-and-mortar business, hiring more staff is a quick fix.

More time to think

As business involves time and money, having more time to concentrate on other things or having more time to think about your next move in business is a huge benefit. Entrepreneurs may want to filter out the noise and think of how to lead their company.

Steps to outsource your business

If you are feeling stressed or overwhelmed, or you want to scale up what you do currently to a new level, then outsourcing is worth a try.

There are many benefits of outsourcing, ranging from more personal freedom, to more profits. To get better results, below is an outline of how to outsource and earn more money.

1. **Define**

The first thing is to figure out what you do, what you want to do, and what you can outsource. Look for a piece of paper and break it down into four columns: What you do, what you hate to do, what you want to do, and what you can delegate. Fill in the details of every column. This may take time, but the first step is necessary to help you understand where you are, and where you want to be.

However, don't be too conservative on the "delegate" list. If you think you can delegate, include it no matter what. Put it there and figure out the details later on.

2. **Decide on what comes first**

Go to the "delegate" column and determine the top 3 things that you need to do most. Identify one that you feel comfortable in delegating immediately. Write down exactly what you want to be done on these things. Outline the action steps that you would follow to do it. Then you can break it down until it reaches a level to which a skilled technician can adhere.

Still, if you have a technical task that you would want to outsource from the column of things you don't like doing, list it down. Don't spend a lot of time on the outline. Find out what you want to do, and write out scenarios in which you may need it.

For example, if you run a web design company, most of the tasks you would want to outsource relate to web development and design. If you don't like coding, you can look for a good coder. Then as you scale down your business, you can hire more people to do the other tasks.

3. Identify

The next step is to interview your ideal employee. The more specific you are, the more qualified applicants you get, and the easier the remaining steps become. Once you are clear about what you want, you will get what you want.

Additionally, the better you define your pool of candidates, the easier the interview will be.

You need to choose:

- The skill areas you need
- The level of skill you need those areas
- The approximate number of hours per week you need to get it done and the number of hours you prefer them to work
- Determine your budget

4. Post your job

Once you figure out your needs, your next immediate tasks, and your ideal candidate, it is time to go to the job boards. Begin by posting a job.

If you want to become rich in outsourcing, your creativity is the only limit. As an individual, you can make use of cheap labor for the most part.

What you earn in a day may be enough to employ another person to work for you in 2 weeks. Don't forget that the tasks you are not very good at, you can decide to outsource and get the work done in a shorter time and at a great price.

Outsourcing is a great thing, and the opportunities are many. If you dream about making money, there are several ideas that you can apply to make money. Just be creative and try to identify good business ideas.

Chapter 20: Make YouTube videos

No kidding, you can make a nice income from YouTube videos. And it may just be the most interesting money-making trick out there.

But it is not as easy as clicking your finger and the money magically showing up in your bank account. Making a lot of money from YouTube videos is still a simple idea.

While you can be lucky to wake up and find that your video has gone viral on the internet, it is a rare thing to happen. In the present world, short, funny videos tend to go viral via Facebook and Twitter rather than YouTube.

You are likely to grow your revenue by getting new audience via constant content publishing, whether it involves creating vlogs, filming your cat, creating a popular video game, or many more.

How much can you make from YouTube?

You have perhaps heard of celebrities making millions of dollars every year from their YouTube channels. However, for most YouTubers, the earnings are modest.

As a standard estimate, you can expect to generate around $1.5 per 1,000 views. But still, the most popular channels and videos can generate between **£6 or £7 per 1,000 views.**

Also, remember that YouTubers and channels normally generate their own merchandise with relevant companies – both of which can add to the income generated from the video views alone.

Marketing contracts, which normally involve posting videos, pay thousands of pounds. And if, say, you can convince your YouTube subscribers to follow you on Instagram, you could even earn more for promoted posts.

Multi-channel networks

If you have done a bit of homework into generating money on YouTube, you may have come across the phrase, "multi-channel networks" (MCNs). As the name implies, MCNs are typically management groups for YouTube channels.

Being a member of MCN can grant you access to better quality products and editing devices, the chance to work together with other YouTube celebrities, plus marketing and growing your channel.

Dangers of MCNs

In exchange for support an MCN provides, you may need to sacrifice a certain percentage of your earnings, and other creative opportunities. This looks fair, but MCNs are considered to abuse their power.

So, while becoming a member of a multi-channel network can be a great way to push your work to the next level, you should never accept to sign a contract that you aren't pleased with. Some of these companies can and have taken advantage of content creators before, and you can end up earning less money than you would than if you had done it alone.

How YouTube Partner Program operates

The YouTube Partner Program (YPP) is a program that allows video creators on the site to begin to monetize content. The members of the program can make money from different sources, including:

- Adverts on your videos
- Channel memberships

- Super chats
- YouTube Premium subscribers

Becoming a member of the program

Unfortunately, you cannot become a member of YPP if you only have one viral video.

Before you become a member, you must ensure you have more than, 1,000 subscribers and your videos must have been watched for a total of over 4,000 hours in the last 12 months. You will still have to respect the community regulations of YouTube.

Once you are in, you will need to sign up for a Google AdSense account. Don't be scared if you think your audience will be put off by ads. You can still choose the types of ads you want to feature on your videos.

And something else that you must know is that you cannot market anything that has a copyrighted resource. Therefore, if you filmed a short section of a certain gig and upload it on YouTube, you will not be able to use it to make money from any ads on this video.

In general, hitting the minimum limit needed to become a member of YPP is a big task.

What do you require to launch a successful YouTube Channel?

Based on what you want to capture on film, you will have to get the right set-up prepared in advance.

There is no need to use your iPhone to record the funniest vlogs ever seen. A great set-up goes a long way towards showing that you are serious and have people respect your videos.

Starter kit for YouTube Channel:

1. A great camera. Quality is vital and you will need to record full 1080p HD videos if you can. If you are looking for a camera, you can go for the Canon G7X, or the Logitech C920, if you prefer to use a camera.

2. Video editing tool. The iMacs have great video editing software, but for PC users who are looking for something advanced, there are other options. You can select Adobe Premier, Final Cut Pro, and VEGAS.

3. Lighting. Spending cash on lighting isn't important, but some top YouTubers prefer it. You can still employ your own creativity, or you can purchase some dedicated video-lighting devices.

4. Microphone. Many cameras come with an inbuilt microphone, but you just want a top sound quality microphone, you may have to fork out some cash and buy a separate one. Based on your budget, you can go for the Blue Snowball, or the Blue Yeti.

5. A decent backdrop. If you are going to film a vlog, you may want to prepare a decent backdrop. You can choose a plain color, or jazz it up by customizing the room you are filming it in to look attractive.

6. Capture card: If you want to record console games, then you only need one of these. If that is what you plan to do, then you can look for the Elgato HD60.

How to shoot the best videos?

As said before, you will not be paid until you become popular, and the more popular you become, the more money you get paid. A bit frustrating as it may sound, it makes sense. You won't be paid to market on a billboard that nobody walks past, so why pay to market on a video that nobody watches?

While creating a better audience may appear hectic, you can still manage to do it alongside your day-to-day life. Below are some top tips to consider:

1. **Stay confident**

Nobody wants to see a person who's afraid to stare at the camera. At the same time, don't be overconfident to the point where it appears cringey. Simply convince your audience to believe that they need to see you.

2. **Follow popular trends**

Focus on what other popular channels are posting, and not just what has done well in the past.

3. **Identify your niche and be unique**

This can look like a contradiction, but being unique is vital. If you do the same thing as someone else, the odds are that people will prefer to watch the person who attains a million views on each video.

Keeping that in mind, take some time to rethink what you do well and whether you think people would be interested in it. Take a look at the popular trends, and figure out what new things you can add.

For instance, gaming videos are quite popular on YouTube, but at the same time, it's a very competitive field to break into. See whether you can think of something unique – if you can, you might have just found your niche.

Other popular trends include comedy, product reviews, general how-to guides – you can think of a way to take advantage of the following trends while remaining unique.

Don't be scared when you begin with a half-baked idea of what you want to do.

4. Select a good channel name

This may appear irrelevant, but it really counts. The first impression on the user is important.

When you want to choose a channel name, take time to review channel names of popular YouTubers to get some inspiration. Keep it unique and attractive.

5. Be yourself

It's one of the best tips for making friends, and to be honest, it applies to all spheres of life. If you try to take on a new persona, you will realize that it is difficult because of it being unbearable and tiring.

And that is not to say the fact that, even if you are a pretty skilled actor, your audience will definitely know that you are faking it.

Pretending to be someone else is a stressful mistake that many YouTubers make.

6. Create catchy, relevant titles and thumbnails

Clickbait is important on YouTube nowadays. In case a video doesn't look attractive from the thumbnail and title, people aren't going to click on it.

Ensure that you have a thumbnail and title that will make your video attractive and make people want to look for more. That said, don't put something that isn't linked to the video or is just a lie. YouTube has caught people for this and banned their channels.

7. **Post regular content**

If you want your channel to become popular and to remain so, you will need to be active often with new content every day.

Whether you choose to post daily, weekly, or monthly videos, upload them at regular intervals. Posting on a particular day every week allows your viewers to maintain track of when some fresh content will come, and probably stop people asking for the next video.

8. **Show people that you love your content**

Becoming yourself isn't enough. Probably the most important thing is to reveal to your viewers that you love whatever you are doing.

Show passion for your videos, and your subject matter. This will create an impact on how they are received. If you look interested, the probability is that your viewers will be interested too.

Alternatively, if you don't like what you are doing, you will soon tire and the videos will start to show that. Remember, passion comes first, and money second.

Always ensure to adhere to the rules too. Don't post wrong content, spamming or copyright. Adhere to the rules of YouTube and you will start to make money soon.

Other methods to make money with YouTube

Affiliate marketing

One of the most available options is to take advantage of affiliate marketing. This was discussed earlier in one of the chapters, but nothing wrong to repeat. Affiliate marketing requires that you post a link to a website, and if another person uses that link to buy something, you get a percentage of the sale.

Sometimes you can also be paid if someone just clicks on the link without buying anything. Affiliate marketing is something that any YouTuber can give a try.

Sponsorship

Popular YouTube channels generate money through sponsorship deals. These deals relate to the content on your channel, but as time goes by, a company can approach you as a move to get its name out there, regardless of the channel.

And don't be worried that you cannot get a sponsorship deal if you aren't at celebrity levels.

If you are at a decent views-per-video level, a sponsor will be ready to pay you a certain amount per video for mentioning the product or featuring the product on the video intro.

If you think you cannot get paid by a promoter, it also good to approach a few companies and see whether they can offer you free sample products in exchange for reviewing them in your video.

As long as you follow the guidelines of advertising, this could be the best way to benefit from your YouTube channel.

Donations

Sites such as Buy Me a Coffee, Patreon, and Ko-fi are powerful tools that will let your fans register and donate money if they would like to support your channel.

You are depending on the goodwill of the people, but if you want to increase your chances of them donating, you can provide them with some exclusive content or products as an appreciation.

The secret to doing well here is to create an audience that will appreciate what you upload. If they like what you do, the probabilities are that they can be convinced to spare some bob every time you upload.

Merchandise

Based on how successful you can be, you can consider branching out and developing your personal merchandise.

Whether it's t-shirts, mugs, or something small like badges or pens, loyal fans will be on alert to participate if they think it makes them become part of the community, and that they are helping you.

Chapter 21: Peer-to-Peer Lending

Peer-to-peer lending is a method to let money earn you more. This method requires that you lend money to others, and when the time of paying back comes, you are paid back with interest. It is not easy to start peer-to-peer lending – you need to first consider many questions that will cross your mind.

Traditionally, when you wanted to purchase a property or a house, you had to depend on the bank to finance you with capital in the form of a loan. The banks were not that reliable because they could either accept or reject you based on the history of your credit, how much salary you make, and the general status of your finances.

Therefore, different sites were created to offer competition to banks. An example of a lending site is the Lending Club (LC). These sites were developed to help anyone who wants to receive a loan. As such, if you were denied by the bank because of a bad credit score, you could look for peer-to-peer lending sites and borrow money. These sites work in such a way that investors contribute money, and later earn a small interest from the money once it is paid back after lending.

Investors find this as a lucrative way to make money because they can lend and earn interest every time it is paid back. While it can be risky to just lend anyone money, Lending Club collects data of borrowers so that they can use it to determine to whom to lend.

Around 50% of LC loans are acquired by people to pay their credit card debt at a lower interest rate. Therefore, Lending Club can be the best place to borrow money to pay your credit card debts.

LC co-operates with defaulters to assist them clear their debts. Based on their record, they have a higher success rate than any other credit card company.

Getting started with peer-to-peer lending –

1. **Set your goals**

Setting your goals is a critical step in any business venture. It is good to have at least three goals for any investment you plan to take part in. Think about the amount of money you want to commit each month, your monthly target for this specific investment, and the place of this investment globally.

After you determine your level of commitment to the investment, you should decide the amount of money your investment should generate on a monthly basis. Try and allocate a certain portion of your monthly salary to invest in the peer-to-peer lending. P2P lending will offer you with an average profit of 10% every year.

2. **Choose a Peer-to-Peer Lending Platform**

Now that you are ready to invest in peer-to-peer lending, you have to look for a great P2P platform. This is not easy, but you need to research well on the available platforms. Look at the ups and downs of every platform. Read some articles and press releases. The point is that you need to be knowledgeable and informed about the platforms you want to invest in. It is quite wrong to invest in a platform which you aren't familiar about.

Also, choose a platform with a great track record of performance. The platform should have a certain percentage of loans available. A site that has only a few loans available may not be a great place to get started.

3. **Invest in your first loan**

Once you decide on the type of platform you want to invest, then invest your first loan. Depending on their payment options, you will have to transfer your money to this platform. Don't worry about this process, because most platforms prefer bank transfers first. Using this payment method, the cash will be available in less than 2 days.

Once the money is in the account, you can proceed to invest in your first loan. Ensure that you make this first investment as peer-to-peer lending. As a new investor, remember to invest the least amount of loan until the time when you gain experience.

4. Switch to Autopilot

After some time, you will have learned the basics, and you can then consider leveling up things and automating the whole system. There are moments when payments will return to your account, and you don't want to re-invest your profits and choose new loans.

Therefore, you need to apply the auto-investing function module provided in the platform. Some of these functions may be opaque, but many will set filters, and the site will invest in any loan that meets your criteria.

For that reason, you must be familiar with the terms of each filter. If not, you won't know how to set the system for automated investing function on the platform you use. Remember that when you start, you have to choose your automated investing function. Once the automation works, you can begin to enjoy your passive income stream from peer-to-peer lending.

5. Monitor your progress

While this last step will not generate income for you, it is still critical for your success. You must monitor your investments. This is important because it will indicate how well your strategy is working. If you have low returns on your investment because most of the loans have defaulted, you have a huge problem.

It is advised to review your P2P lending accounts per month. The platform will always show your current profit on investment. Be alert – these numbers are just an approximation, and you may have to use accurate techniques to identify your initial return on investment. However, to start with, the numbers created in the platform are enough.

In case you see your profits go lower than what the platform advertises, this is the period to return to the first stage and arrange your plan. Monitoring your progress will direct you to know whether you have attained some goals, and whether you can set new goals to go to the next level.

Chapter 22: Private Equity Investing

Many investors prefer to use the traditional channel of investing by purchasing stocks or bonds, and sometimes, a mutual fund or two. But for some, private equity is an attractive investment route. Additionally, it can be a great way of earning passive income.

Definition of private equity

"Private equity" is a general term used to refer to all types of funds that collect money from a group of investors to accumulate millions of dollars that are later used to earn stakes in companies. So in short, private equities are shares of ownership that aren't publicly traded. As a result, private equity is developed through private equity companies.

When developing private equity, investors will produce capital to invest in private companies – they can either support mergers and acquisitions, facilitate the stability of a company's balance sheet, contribute new capital, or activate new projects. And this capital is usually contributed by institutional investors.

Some of the major operations of private equity firms consist of buying out financially-challenged companies and making them better by restructuring. You can also invest directly in companies and allow mergers once a healthy return is created.

How private equity is controlled

Since private equity is regulated by active firms that want to sell, fix, or affect companies, private equity managers are in a great position. Same as other investment firms, private equity is controlled by managers that deal with assets under management within firms. The private equity firms and funds depend on the investors' money to purchase large companies to optimize profit. They have the best professionals in law, accounting, and from the 500 Global Fortune Companies list. But most of the private equity firms have a modest number of employees, with some hiring less than two dozen associates.

While the fee structure isn't same across the board, private equity firms have performance and management fees, both of which boast of 20 percent of gross profits at the time of sale and 2 percent on controlled assets.

Since private equity firms are smaller than investment funds, it is a great chance to get a job in these firms. Managers of private equity always work hand-in-hand with partners of the firm and are always requested to manage the firm's portfolios.

How to launch your own private equity fund?

Private equity firms have been a successful asset and the sector continues to expand as more portfolio managers take part in the industry. Most investment bankers have switched from public to private equity because of their good performance in the last couple of decades. Currently, there is a huge demand for private equity firms, and new managers have to come out and offer investors new opportunities to invest their money.

Nowadays, there are a lot of successful private equity firms – however, most of them are small-to-mid-sized and can have a range of 2-100 employees. Here are steps you can follow to start your own private equity fund:

Define a business strategy

First, you must detail your business plan and distinguish it from competitors. Building a business plan requires in-depth research into a specific market or individual sector. Some funds concentrate on energy development, while others concentrate on early-stage biotech companies. In general, investors will want to understand much about your fund's goal.

As you define your strategy, think about whether you will have a geographic focus: Will the funds lean on one side? Will it concentrate on a different industry in another nation? Or it will it talk about a certain strategy in a developing market?

That aside, there are various business focuses you can involve in. Will your fund try to boost your portfolio company's operation, or will this depend fully on cleaning their balance sheets?

Keep in mind that private equity affects investment companies that don't trade on the public market. It is important that you define the focus of every investment. For instance, is the objective of the investment to expand the capital for acquisitions and mergers? Or is the plan to generate capital that will let existing owners sell their position in the company?

Streamline the business plan and operations

The second step requires that you create a business plan, which determines cash flow expectations, the timeline of your private equity funds, and many more. Every fund has a life period of about 10 years. A solid business plan has a procedure on the money that will increase with time, as well as a marketing strategy.

Once you create a business plan, you must set up an external team of consultants that features an independent accountant, and an industry personnel who can deliver insight into the industries of the companies in your portfolio. It is also prudent to set up an advisory team and look at disaster-recovery methods of steep market downturns.

Another useful step is to set up the firm and come up with the name of the firm. In addition, the manager has to make a decision on the roles and titles of those who will lead the firm. From there on, create the management team. First-time managers have higher odds of generating more money if they come from a successful firm.

On the other side, it is necessary to define in-house operations. Some of these operations include rent, technology requirements, furniture, and hiring members. There are many other things to put into consideration when employing staff.

Determine the investment path

Once early operations have been made, determine the legal structure of the fund. In the USA, a fund often takes the structure of a restricted firm. Since you are the creator of the fund, you will be a general partner – in other words, you will have permission to choose the investment that has the fund.

Your investors will be restricted associates who don't have the permission to choose the companies that belong to your fund. Partial partners are only involved in the losses related to their discrete investment, while general partners will deal with extra losses within the fund.

All in all, your attorney will create a private placement agreement and any other agreements needed.

The downside

Start-ups in the early stages have challenges to integrate into private equity investment plans. Additionally, keep in mind that a private equity fund's goal is to increase the value of the company, so that they can ensure their investors make returns on investments.

Chapter 23: Real Estate Crowdfunding

Crowdfunding is a new interesting method for real estate investors to create capital. Well, how does it work? What are some of the advantages of crowdfunding real estate deals? What things should you be aware of while searching for a real estate investment loan? What profits could you get by investing in different crowdfunding projects?

While real estate crowdfunding isn't a traditional method of generating capital, it is good for investors to be aware of this powerful means of real estate financing.

Real estate crowdfunding – what is it?

Crowdfunding is a method whereby the business generates money by reaching out to a large pool of investors who contribute a certain amount of cash. The main difference between crowdfunding and traditional methods of generating money is that the platform for crowdfunding is available online.

Together with crowdfunding websites, owners of the business can depend on social media platforms like Twitter and Facebook, etc., to promote their ventures directly to a large audiences of interested investors.

Real estate investors have employed crowdfunding as an alternative means to more traditional methods of financing investments. Many developers are applying crowdfunding platforms to get investments from groups of approved investors, while small business owners have started campaigns to collect funds for smaller deals.

Advantages of crowdfunding for real estate

No matter where you are in your real estate journey, having the necessary financing to support a deal can be challenging. With its emergence in the real estate industry, most investors have used crowdfunding as a means to fund deals. In addition, crowdfunding is tied in with different advantages, including:

- Crowdfunding a real estate property boosts the funding choices while expanding the investor network.
- Successful projects will result in a positive word of mouth and client loyalty.
- Save money and time by utilizing user-friendly investment platforms.
- Get access to helpful feedback from the online community so that you can address the business challenges.

Easy access to capital

Crowdfunding grants access to credit and capital. In this case, it saves a person the hassle of looking for a loan in the bank. In addition, it is applied in any type of fundraising one can think of: Personal, family, business and real estate investing. Investors can gain by storing their personal credit free and available for other functions.

This lets small business owners run their companies quickly, and assist investors to protect funding for deals when more traditional options are restricted.

A better marketing tool

Besides the direct benefit of funding, crowdfunding is an excellent marketing tool for business owners who want to market their niche.

By creating crowdfunding campaigns via social networks and directly on crowdfunding sites, investors of real estate have a chance to quickly grow their investor network. The best method is to offer a credibility package on your site, displaying past projects and profits, plus the mission of your company and its objectives. This increases the confidence and credibility among interested investors.

Develops investor loyalty

A crowdfunding campaign is an excellent strategy to showcase the attractive side and financial viability of a project. By providing compelling information via the campaign process, you attract prospective investors and gain support. Once you protect your funding, the people who contribute will invest in your success and will move forward to help you succeed. By offering regular results, your investors will achieve a sense of loyalty, which can result in a positive word-of-mouth promotion.

User-friendly ground available

Many real estate crowdfunding platforms will simplify the process for investors to start their fundraising campaigns. As a result, this saves them time and money. These sites are developed to illustrate campaigns in an attractive manner while letting fundraisers interact with a large audience without much effort.

Gain important feedback

Because of the public nature of crowdfunding, the campaigns will be subject to reactions, with or without invitation. But this is a huge chance for business owners to track user comments and acquire feedback. For instance, focus on the feedback left by experienced investors, even if it is criticisms. Responding and appreciating users for sparing their time to reach out can assist you to open up lines of communication and build genuine connections with new contacts.

Also, it is necessary to identify if there is a learning curve for those who haven't taken part in crowdfunding. When you start your first campaign, some of the feedback discussed here will help you to learn how you can improve your campaign. It can also be a huge chance to introduce the idea of crowdfunding to those people who aren't familiar with it.

Making money with real estate crowdfunding

As defined before, real estate crowdfunding is when you raise money with other investors to purchase real estate property.

This gives you the opportunity to invest in real estate with the least amount of money you have. You will then own a fraction of the multi-million real estate projects.

Developers tend to use crowdfunded money to construct projects. And investors earn profits via rental income, or when the value of the property appreciates.

Real estate crowdfunding is an amazing method to earn passive income. The professionals handle everything for you and manage the properties on your behalf. Your role is just to wait for returns.

Ideally, investors get paid in two ways:

- **Dividends:** This is income created from the properties, either via interest, rent or mortgage. The dividends are a means to generate passive income. Pay attention if the site distributes dividends quarterly or monthly.

- **Rise in the value of the shares**: This happens when the property increases in value. You get paid at the end of the investment when the property is sold. This can occur after some years.

That said, it is important to know that there are two categories of crowdfunding projects:

- Equity: This occurs when you own the real estate property. Returns are computed through profits. This is a bit risky, but there is a higher return.

- Debt: In this case, you act as the lender. Returns will be collected through lending money at a fixed rate of interest. This has a lower risk, but the returns are fixed.

Reasons to use a real estate crowdfunding platform

- **You can invest with as little as $5:** Since you collect your funds together with other investors, you don't need thousands of dollars to invest in real estate. You can still invest in real estate that would not always be accessible.

- **Portfolio diversification:** Investing in real estate offers you the ability to diversify – you can invest in stocks and bonds. This will help you overcome the challenges that the market experiences.

- **Understand your upfront risk:** Many crowdfunding platforms offer details of the investment upfront, plus the percentage of risk and expected returns.

- **Invest in most projects:** Rather than just invest in a single real estate project, your money can be invested in different other projects in the USA. This will spread the risk in case a particular area experiences a downturn.

- **Tax advantage:** Real estate investments are always created using taxable accounts, but an investor can apply a self-directed IRA account to invest in real estate.

Things to consider in a real estate crowdfunding opportunity

- **Income requirements:** This is one of the largest limiting factors in sites and investment options.

- **The least investment amount:** Can you fulfill the platform's minimum investment requirement?

- **Investment options:** Do you want equity or debt? Do you want to make more passive income now or in the future? Each carries its own risk, possible profits, and fees. Select a platform that provides what you need for your goals.

- **A transparent process:** You can have access to all the details of the investments to make a quality decision.

- **The time horizon of the investments:** In general, real estate investment is illiquid. So, if you aren't comfortable for your funds to be tied up for years, search for platforms with a shorter project timeline.

- **A comprehensive evaluation procedure:** Check out how well the company interviews every developer and their certification criteria.

Real estate crowdfunding creates a unique opportunity to take part in real estate without emerging with large sums of cash.

Chapter 24: Rent Out a Room

Another month has come and ended, and you have just paid your mortgage, although you struggled to get that money. So you relax a bit, but soon the worries come back regarding the bills of the next month.

If you are familiar with this scenario, you aren't the only one. Many people face similar scenarios. At the start of every month, they begin to think of where they will find money to clear their various bills.

They quickly search for other ways to clear their expenses for buying food. It is a stressing and uncomfortable situation.

Luckily, there is light at the end of the tunnel. Many homeowners that are struggling have resorted to renting out a room in their homes to assist them to meet their needs in life. While this looks like a sudden move, renting a house to strangers is something that started to happen a long time ago. Renting out your room is an easy means to reduce the burden to pay bills.

In addition, this can be a great way to add some extra income on top of what you earn in your 9-5 job. Well, how can you land a great tenant? How do you deal with the different housing laws? First, let's briefly consider the pros and cons of renting a house:

Pros and cons

Sharing your home with a person with whom you have no family ties has its own ups and downs. Consider the following advantages and drawbacks before you move forward to rent out your room:

Pros

Of course, the most important advantage is that the rental income you get will allow you to reduce your mortgage bill. The extra money you receive you can use to pay your credit card debt, and any other loan you may have. Whatever you choose to do with the rent, renting out a room gives you additional cash that you can use to pay outstanding bills.

Depending on the agreement you have with the tenant, you can benefit by letting the renter chip in certain household duties. In return, he or she gets a small cut in the rent. Sometimes, renting out a room in a house where you live alone gives you peace of mind because you now know you aren't alone in the home.

Cons

The biggest challenge that comes when you rent out a room in your home is safety. You don't really know much about the person going to stay in your home. Letting a stranger to stay in your home may make your family members feel uncomfortable. You could be worried that they will steal some of your possessions, or even invite thieves in.

It is not easy to find someone you can trust and a person whom you share many values. For example, you could be a quiet person who sleeps early, but if you find a person who loves to listen to loud music and sleeps late, you will be much disturbed.

The steps to renting out a room

Even after reading through the pros and cons, letting in a tenant is still an excellent choice. Below is a list of steps that you need to take for a memorable experience:

1. **Determine the local laws and HOA rules**

This is the first step that you need to do. You must familiarize yourself with the tenant laws and ordinances in your city. Keep in mind that these laws differ based on the city you are in.

2. Speak with your insurance agency

Once you have been cleared to rent a room in your home, next is to check if your homeowner insurance policy grants access to it. There are companies that have no problem with this, while others forbid renting sections of your home. Other companies will not increase the rate if you rent to a tenant, but some will go ahead to increase the rate.

When you rent out your room, you tend to increase the risk of property damage. This means that your insurance company may decide to revoke your coverage. If this happens to you, the next thing to do is to seek for landlord insurance. This can cost between 15% - 20% more than the insurance of homeowners.

3. Select the room to rent

Once everything is okay, you can start to consider the details. Think of the design of your home. You may decide to sleep in the master bedroom and rent out the additional room, or rent out the master bedroom and move to the extra room. If you rent out a master bedroom, you will possibly charge more than what you would have asked for the additional room. Whichever option you go for, make sure it is the best option for both you and the tenant.

4. Determine the price

Before you publish the price on an ad, it is good to compare with rental rates of neighboring areas to get a rough idea of how much you can charge for your room. Here, you can opt to use sites like Rentometer, or Craigslist.

5. Create a strategic listing

Nowadays, the services of Roomster, Roommates, and SpareRoom simplify the process of finding the right tenants depending on their taste. You can liken it to online dating. The sites mentioned above will grant you the ability to market your room and categorize your prospective tenants based on their online profile.

While creating a list, publish quality photos that capture the best view of the room. Don't exaggerate anything. Post pictures of the house plus any other thing you think is important.

6. Adhere to the Federal and State Housing Laws

While you vet applicants, familiarize yourself with the housing rules to save yourself from hurting a tenant. Use a genuine and certified Credit Reporting Agency to ensure that you respect the Fair Housing Act (FHA), which is in place to restrict house discrimination.

Maintain your approval process:

The FHA forbids discrimination where the homeowner serves one type of person differently than the other.

For instance, if you secretly don't want to let a single mother in your room, then you discover that one of the applicants is a single mom, so you demand that she has a higher credit score than other applicants, and then you turn her down because her score isn't sufficient. The FHA standards forbid this kind of behavior.

Or, say, you don't want pets in your home. Then one of the applicants has a service dog and you deny him because of the "no pets policy." According to the FHA, you would have broken the rules.

So you see why you need to spare some time and understand the fair housing laws? You will also have to screen your tenants – this will protect you just in case a tenant files a discrimination case against you. You can create a form that you will use to screen your tenants. This form should contain everything that you need to look for in a tenant when vetting potential tenants. Of course, it is an added task to create this particular form, but it can assist you to avoid paying a fine of $16,000 if you fail to provide a solid defense. This penalty doesn't include the money you will have to pay the attorney or the court. Penalties often rise up quickly after the first offense, so you should ensure that you comply with the law when screening tenants. If you don't know how to create a tenant screening form, you can search for free samples online.

Though you need to be careful while vetting potential tenants, there is leeway: It is possible for you to be excluded from the FHA, in particular, if you are the owner of the home you are living in, and it has less than four rental units.

7. Ask the correct questions

Once you know what you need to do, ensure that you ask your tenant relevant questions. If you don't know the type of questions you can ask a tenant, you can consider the questions below during the time of the interview.

- What is the reason for moving?
- Where are you living in currently?
- Which date would you prefer to move in?
- For how long are you going to rent?
- Are you going to live with someone?
- Where do you work?
- Do you smoke?

- Have you ever faced an eviction?
- Will you pass a credit check?

All the questions listed above are okay to ask. However, specific things must be addressed properly. For example, while you cannot directly ask if an applicant has a family, you can ask whether they will be moving in with anyone. But ensure that you review the Fair Housing Act information so that you don't risk a lawsuit by asking invalid questions.

8. Do a background check

Once you vet potential tenants and identified one whose personality seems compatible with yours, the next step is a background check. There are different degrees of background checks right from a credit check to a comprehensive criminal record check.

No matter the type of report you decide to use, the Fair Credit Reporting Act demands that you use the Consumer Reporting Agency (CRA). This report helps protect both the tenant and the landlord.

If you reject a prospective tenant based on a given aspect you come across in their background check, you have to tell them a reason. The landlord must provide the tenant with comprehensive information.

So be detailed on why you are rejecting them and provide them the contact information of a firm you used to get a report that has helped you find a reason to reject them. Additionally, this company must obey the Fair Credit Reporting Act, or else you will face a serious fine or even jail time if you are sued by the person you rejected.

9. Claim rental income on your taxes

Remember that the rental income you earn is taxable. The amount you will send as a marginal tax rate will vary. You will have to pay both the state and local taxes on the following income.

In addition, you should indicate any services you get from your tenant in exchange for rent on your taxes.

10. Remove your expenses

When you rent a section in your home, you can remove any costs you suffered to renovate the room. This will include all repairs, upgrades and many more. You need to also exclude the costs you suffer for the whole home. But then you must divide the expenses by the square footage of the room you are renting out.

For example, in a 2,000 square feet home where 400 square feet is rented out, equals 20% of the total square footage of the home. In this case, exclude 20% of the home upgrades, repairs, or expenses like:

- Mortgage insurance
- Painting
- Utilities like water, gas, and electricity
- Roofing repairs
- Trash removal
- Security system costs

11. Set the boundary and authenticate the lease

Once you get a tenant that you want and know who you can trust, define your boundaries on the first day. Develop a lease agreement, sign the lease and let the tenant also sign it. This will define the details of your living room.

For example, will the tenant pay the monthly rental fee or also a certain percentage of the utilities? Where will the food be kept? What permission does your boarder have to other places in the living area? Are pets allowed? What about night visitors?

All these things must be discussed and agreed to before your tenant moves in.

Lastly, search for a security deposit and define the types of damages that will make the tenant lose their deposit. Make sure you research the housing laws of your state to ensure that you don't charge too much for a security deposit.

12. Secure your properties

With time, you will start to learn more about your tenant, and you will begin to see that he or she is trustworthy and you could leave behind your valuables without worrying. But until this time comes, makes sure you secure your valuable items. Secure any documents that may put you at risk for identity theft.

13. Respect their space

Once the tenant moves in with his or her items, don't invade their room without permission. Show the same respect to your tenant and you will earn it back as you enjoy your rental income at the end of the month.

While renting a room in your place of residence may appear a severe move, it's now popular for most homeowners who want to earn an extra income. With the right organization and preparation, it can be an interesting means of saving money for both parties.

Chapter 25: Rent Out Your Furniture

Someone may have told you about making money by flipping furniture as a passive income stream. It's an attractive business if your target is to make more money than you do now. Everyone likes the idea of making some extra bucks as a side hustle. This can be really helpful if you are living in a lucrative city.

Getting started with a rental business can be a very appealing venture. But, before you start the business, you will have to carry out a feasibility study and market research on the current level of competitiveness. This will help you to know how viable the idea of rental furniture business is. Make sure that you have a solid business plan in place, which will not just guide you in running the business, but act as a great piece of evidence to get a loan. Create policies to guide you on the payment gateway, rates, terms, and many more. This will curb any conflict that may occur. Confirm with the local and federal authorities to learn more about the relevant permits, taxation, and licenses needed to start a furniture business.

To ensure that your business runs smoothly, you should not let prices go beyond a certain level. Therefore, you should take advantage of major selling points such as variety, flexibility, quality, and delivery. A furniture business will involve some work and time. As such, you must be patient to be able to see it succeed. Below are points to consider when starting a furniture rental business:

1. **Choose your niche well**

It is important that you identify a direction for your business. Since there are many different types of rental furniture businesses, you must choose your niche and identify what you want to sell. This can range from baby furniture, luxury furniture, executive furniture, to basic home furniture.

Likewise, home furniture is further divided into kitchen, living, and bedroom furniture. This will not only assist to set up an identity for yourself, but it will provide you with a specific target market. Next, you can start to make arrangements for your marketing, operations, and promotions around the target market.

2. Identify a retail store

Although you can manage the furniture business from your home, finding a great office space is important. Try to get retail space in a commercial ground. If you can get an office close to shops of home supplies, it can provide you with great visibility and more customers. If your rental furniture can be used by students, make sure that you have an outlet near the university dorms. If you are going to lease out office furniture, look for a store where offices nearby are on rent.

3. Legal contract

You will need to seek the help of your lawyer to create a rental contract that will outline the terms of leasing out the furniture. This will involve the leasing date, return date, total period before the due date, repair policy, payment terms, compensation for destruction policy, late payment, and many more. Both parties will have to say yes to the terms and include their signature. This is a vital step because a legal contract is evidence of the agreement between you and the renter.

4. Sourcing finance

You will need a certain amount of money to purchase the different types of furniture, store it in a warehouse, and hire a company to facilitate transport. If you don't have the required savings, you can seek an SBA loan or a bank loan. You can also find out whether any business incubators are available in your area. This will help you to save cost and offer support. In addition, you can present a credit union loan if you are one of their members. This will assist you to get funds at lower interest rates.

5. Look for a warehouse

You will need to find a warehouse space to keep your furniture until the time a person comes to hire it. Make sure that the warehouse is big enough to accommodate all your furniture. Don't end up stacking one on top of the other one. This can easily destroy the furniture and increase your cost of repair and maintenance. Additionally, make sure that there are no rodents living in the warehouse. Rodents are dangerous because they will eat away the foam. Prevent any rodents' destruction by buying pest control and applying it in the space. Also, search for any molds on walls which can reach your furniture and damage it. Besides this, it is important that you put up your furniture in a place that is well secured. If you think space is a problem, you can consider putting it in a garage. However, this will be insecure because someone can come and steal your furniture. Lastly, remember to check the insurance of the warehouse.

6. Hire or purchase moving trucks

You will need to arrange transport for the furniture to the doorstep of the customer. So you will have to look for moving trucks and some labor to help carry the furniture to the trucks. At the start, it is advised that you hire a moving truck. Over time, it will prove to be quite expensive. Once your business stabilizes, start to plan on buying your own moving truck and add another one when it continues to grow. You can also employ people who will help move the furniture.

7. Online showroom

For you to catch the attention of customers, try to create an interactive website which will display the different types of furniture that will be available for purchase. Since it is not possible to go with all the customers to the warehouse to see the furniture, this website will work well for your business. You can also showcase different photos of furniture types, similar options for their selection, number of furniture available, charges for hire, and colors as per duration. Also, get a rent calculator that will show an estimated amount a customer will pay to get a specific type of furniture. If you like, you can offer online booking and payments. This additional feature will help you get many clients.

8. **Sourcing furniture**

You are advised to look for quality furniture for your rental business. As a result, you can set up a wholesale account with a wholesaler to save cost because retail outlets will charge more. You can still decide to go for cheap furniture available on online furniture websites. But if you have plans to go for secondhand furniture, make sure that it is quality furniture, and in good condition. You can still improve it so that it looks attractive and new. However, don't spend money on something that looks used, has stains, and is tattered. Nobody will pay you well if you rent furniture of low quality.

9. **Assess the furniture**

Once the furniture is returned after you have rented it out for a specific period, perform some checks. If you discover that the renter's cat has clawed on the leather sofa, or it has some stains on it, let the renter pay you for damage. Additionally, assess all the metallic and woodworks of the furniture as people like to join the broken legs of chairs using adhesives. Check your furniture thoroughly to identify any small problems. If you discover something missing, damaged or spoiled, then add it to the renter's bill.

10. **Packing**

Once you get the furniture back, you will need to clean, sanitize, and then wrap it properly for storage. If the sofa covers need to be washed, don't be afraid to spend some money on them. A customer will be happy if the furniture smells nice and has the look of a new sofa. Thus, don't forget to pack it well. If you find that any type of repairs is needed for the furniture, conduct it before you lease it out again. Make sure that the furniture is very clean before you rent it out.

11. Business expansion

There are a lot of furniture rental businesses that employ a rent-to-own model for generating profit and have made it. Once you make enough revenue, plan for this strategy and throw your efforts in it to rake more profit. This will also help the renter to use the furniture and purchase it when he can manage. But you should be careful that the people who prefer this method should purchase the furniture once they rent it for a specific period. There are many people who go for used furniture sitting idle in the streets. But they are very sensitive about getting things like mattresses, futons, and couches from unknown places. Therefore, you should consider adding these items to your business to increase your profit.

12. Calculating expenses

Let's say you have spent around $5,000 on a sofa and you are charging $500 per year for renting it out. This will mean that your initial investment will require 10 years to recover, so you need to forget the profit connected to it. In this case, you have to increase the charges such that you will earn a decent profit and recover your investment amount more quickly. Also, if you provide doorstep delivery, remember to include the logistic charges. Unlike cash loan, you cannot run a credit check on a customer. Therefore, you are taking a bigger risk. Thus, you should try to earn a higher amount as a deposit to secure your furniture. Additionally, in case of damage to the furniture by the customer, you can deduct these charges from the deposit.

13. Marketing your business

When it comes to marketing your business, sign up with relevant online websites. You can advertise your business in directories, newspapers, magazines, and many more. Try to be a BBB member and get a nice grade. Also, take advantage of your moving trucks by branding them with promotional ads. Besides that, you can also run your business in social media style and market it.

It is advised that you seek a franchise, or purchase an established business to avoid the many challenges that faces a start-up. Another reason is that it comes with a solid customer base, established set-up, and reputation. All these will help you make huge profits. Since your business depends on the furniture you rent, it is good to take insurance to cover it.

Furniture flipping

This is also another type of business that you can decide to run to supplement your rental furniture business. Let's assume that you have bought furniture at a certain point in your life – you can easily explain why rotten furniture doesn't sell that much. Sellers can increase the price of furniture because of the durability of the wood, or some other factor, but it is difficult to look past the worn out condition of the furniture.

People like the type of furniture they pay for to look squeaky clean and new, and this is where the idea of furniture flipping comes in.

A great furniture flipper can tell what a piece of furniture will look once some work is done on it. People also prefer anything that is customized according to their needs, and if you can master how to customize furniture in an attractive way, you have a great chance to make more money than you make from renting your furniture.

Below are 6 easy ways that will help you to get started with furniture flipping:

Step 1: Understand more about quality

Simply put, landing a great piece of furniture is not the end of everything. If you have the goal of making a profit, then you need to master something about quality. For example, the piece of furniture should be made of real wood. This will help you to save money, which may otherwise be spent elsewhere on re-staining furniture made with fake wood.

You will also want a piece of furniture that is in the right shape so that you don't spend a lot of time repairing it. In other words, look for a piece of furniture that doesn't need a lot of investment, so that you can have a bigger chance to sell it and make a big profit.

Step 2: Learn more about refinishing

Refinishing a piece of furniture to make it look neat and attractive is an important selling point. You can spare some time and look at furniture sale sites for the latest trends. In addition, conduct some research on popular colors and techniques.

You can master something on reupholstering furniture. This is a long process, but you can avoid it by buying furniture pieces that don't need upholstery services.

Ensure you use quality sealers and paints to refinish your furniture. Creating a quality product has a lot to do with quality supplies. If you replace things like pulls and knobs, ensure you purchase a long-lasting type.

Using cheap supplies tend to affect the general quality of the final piece, and will pull down your price.

Step 3: Shop for furniture that can be flipped

Although it is necessary to learn about the quality and refinishing, you still need to have knowledge of where you can find the best pieces of furniture to flip. Some of the best places to hunt for furniture include:

Estate sales

An estate sale is a good starting ground for cheap furniture. People normally hold an estate sale with the idea of selling everything, so items are normally priced at a reasonable price.

Garage sales

You can still find great pieces to flip at a garage sale so you should ensure that you hit all of them in the summer. You can bargain on the price and try to get a discount. If you are planning for this option, remember that you are likely to get a better chance of buying a nice piece if you go on the first day.

Craigslist

Sites like Craigslist and Letgo are great places for purchasing furniture that can later be flipped. The rates are relatively cheap, and you can get many pieces that can be restored.

Flea markets

Flea markets also provide the best options for furniture that can be flipped. The prices are still reasonable though it can take time to get good pieces.

You can also look at furniture pieces where your friends or family members may be eliminating. Another option is to look at the roadside. You will be surprised at how much furniture you can get on the curbside that can be restored and sold at a good profit.

Finding the best furniture to flip is great, but if you don't have a clear plan of how you are going to restore them and what the finished product will look like, it is advisable that you don't move forward and buy the furniture. Or else, you may end up buying furniture where the restored piece doesn't look good. You can take time to think about how you can paint the piece, and the types of pulls that would work for it. This will also help you to see whether or not the piece is restorable.

Step 4: Set up a Facebook page

Facebook is a popular social network for selling items online. Once you have a few flipped furniture, create a Facebook business page to sell and rent your products. Take awesome photos of refinished pieces. Great pictures will attract customers to come to buy or rent your pieces. Next, advertise your work and your sales to create value. Ask your friends to share your products and increase your odds of making a sale. This is an important part of your furniture-flipping business.

Step 5: Organize customer service and choose delivery options

Great customer service can really decide the future of your business. While most people care about the quality of the product, they also focus on the overall customer experience of purchasing from you. It will also boost your odds of making repeat sales so ensure you set a timeline, stick to it, and deliver whatever you promised.

Making decisions on delivery options is another big step.

You can either decide to deliver the furniture or allow your customers to come for it directly. Getting your pieces delivered is likely to increase the number of customers, but it can also be quite expensive and inconvenient. Making sure that the furniture arrives safely without any damage during delivery is still important.

Step 6: Accepting custom orders

Once the furniture flipping business is set up, and you have polished the process of buying, refinishing and selling flipped pieces, you can start to think of accepting custom orders.

These can be highly profitable and also assist you to grow your customer base. Avoid accepting orders that you know you cannot deliver. This can have a serious negative effect. Always ensure that you stay upfront with your customer base if there is something that you know you cannot deliver. Setting the right expectations will save you from headaches.

Generating money by renting out furniture and flipping furniture can be a very profitable business. If you enjoy working with worn-out furniture pieces to make them look neat and attractive as if they are new, there is a lot of opportunity in this business for you. You can even turn it from a passive income stream to a full-time job, and quit your day job when everything stabilizes. Besides making more money, it can be fun.

Chapter 26: Retail Arbitrage/Dropshipping

Dropshipping is an e-commerce business technique where you can sell physical items without getting involved with the inventory, without owning a warehouse to store your items, and without the hustle of dealing with shipping and handling products.

In addition, you don't incur any upfront cost. You don't need to invest money on inventory. Another thing that you will need to have is a website with free credit card processing.

Theoretically, dropshipping looks like a great idea because it is scalable without you doing most of the work upfront. But when you dive deep, there are some complications that you need to know about.

Many people try to start a dropship shop with expectations it is going to be easy, but the truth is, there is more to it than what you think.

How to make passive income with dropshipping

Just like any other type of business, it takes courage, perseverance and good luck to make money. But there are a few actionable insights that you need to consider to help you make a profit from dropshipping:

1. **Understand the pricing**

One of the leading reasons why many people who start a dropshipping business don't succeed is because they don't do enough research on the pricing. Every business requires adequate research before getting started. With dropshipping, you are free to decide on your own prices for your stock, but how can you tell that you are overcharging your buyers or even charging too little?

Many people who run dropshipping business find their stock from websites such as AliExpress, Salehoo, and many other wholesale dropshipping companies where the prices are near to wholesale. This gives you the chance to sell the product at a market price and make a good profit.

Let's say that you want to sell a flashlight that is sold at $5 from AliExpresss. For you to tell how much you are going to sell the product, you have to do some math. First, determine the amount of cash you are going to spend on advertisement, administrative costs, handling, and the store. Once you have compiled this, you will come up with a figure of how much you need to charge. For an item that costs $5, you need to charge around $20 to earn a decent profit.

Once you have finished your research, shift your attention to the competition. They could be selling at a lower price because there are many dropshippers comfortable with a lower margin. Don't be scared – as long as you know you are charging a fair price that is near the market value, you should be safe.

Finally, you can drop your price margins on some products and increase it elsewhere, aiming to increase your general profit. It takes some time to identify the correct pricing for your products, but the only method you can learn from is by measuring out your ideas practically.

2. **Be aware of the items you are selling**

One of the first mistakes of dropshipping is selling the wrong items. Many owners of the store choose products from their niche that they find attractive, rather than focusing on what can sell and make a profit. It is better to hover around on AliExpress and find out the number of reviews a product gets and whether there is a real market for it.

The next mistake that many dropshippers make is selling something which they haven't yet used or tried out. This is probably a dangerous thing. You will be depending on the supplier to tell the truth on their product description and images.

Although you want to save time and money by selling, you should consider purchasing a sample as a necessary development cost. You will receive honest feedback and you will know whether the product is of good quality or not.

You can also save time by reading reviews. Once you are logged into a supplier website, scan through the products and reviews. First, make sure that there are numerous reviews – at least 100. Next, make sure that the average score is near to 5 stars.

Lastly, be creative. Look for products that aren't easily found in the local stores. You need to provide something special for a particular niche that will make visitors want to buy from them. If it is an item that is easy to find, even at the lowest price, buyers won't be interested to buyt because they can get it locally instead of from an online store.

3. Avoid leaning on suppliers

Suppliers are the life wire of any dropshipping business and employing the right one can either make or break your e-commerce shop. Once dropshippers identify a supplier that works responsibly, provides great communication and maintains consistency, they will stick to that supplier.

But it is good to have backups and insurance. The current market is unpredictable, and a reliable supplier can drop off the market in a short time. On the flip side, they can stop selling the item that is highly profitable for your store. No matter the reason, it is advised to have more than one option available, especially when things go wrong.

You may have a different problem altogether – a supplier that is regularly missing the mark. They could be shipping items that don't match the description, or different from what the customer ordered. They may ship damaged products, or use different shipping methods than what is promised, or sometimes postpone the delivery.

In any case, if something like this happens, you need to drop the supplier from your store immediately before they completely damage your business. It's easy to refund a customer, but bad reviews are difficult to handle.

4. **Create an eye-catching website**

Once you step foot in a brick-and-mortar store, the first thing you will see is the appearance of the store. Whether the items are organized, the space is clean, the salesperson is social, friendly and helpful. The same thing goes with your e-commerce store. If the store isn't presentable, not even the best goods at the lowest prices will help your sale.

First, ensure that the general website design looks presentable. There are a lot of Shopify and WordPress theme combinations that may provide you with a decent presentation. But for you to get it right the first time, it's important to employ a designer to handle all the work for you. Take a look at the competition and see what works and what can be improved, and then use that to create a better website.

The second thing that is necessary is the content. Now that your website is set up, it is time to fill it with content. Having a website alone isn't enough until you populate it with the correct content. There is nothing worse than getting into a page with placeholder images and text. Make sure that you have product photos from the first day. You can request your supplier to use their photos, but it is a great idea to request a product first to test it out and take some great photos of them, yourself.

Secondly, all the products should feature relevant, unique and accurate descriptions. This will not only assist in making more sales, but it will also be useful for SEO purposes.

Apart from the standard pages like Home and Product pages, ensure you include other pages like About Us, Shipping, FAQ, and Contract.

5. Be present

The main reason why dropship owners take part in business is to gain enough freedom and quit from their 9-5 job. But running any business requires time and effort.

Even when you have a well-built and stable system, you must be active on your store for at least an hour per day. You must process your orders and notify your suppliers. Customers will come in with questions that you must address as soon as possible, so make sure that you spend less than a day to reply to all questions.

Lastly, you need to monitor your competition closely. No need to commit hours to this on a daily routine, but it is a good thing to check out their social media channels and website. You will get an idea as to what works, and what you can implement better.

6. Learn marketing

As mentioned previously, there are better means to automate your store. Right from processing orders to publishing new social media posts, technology has got you covered. With that in mind, you can concentrate on other urgent issues.

Visitors and buyers won't notice your website on their own, and it is your role to look for ways to attract your audience. One of the easiest methods of attracting a crowd is creating paid ads. Whether it's via PPC advertising or paid social media ads, you will manage to get exactly those people who are in the market looking for your products.

There are complex targeting ways to attaining your desired audiences, but you will need to know your audience in the first place.

However, creating paid ads isn't a long-term method, as you will have to set aside huge amounts of cash for marketing. Keep in mind that although ads can get many visitors, you still need to have a good mastery to know the kinds of ads to run and how to run them.

Alternatively, there is SEO and content marketing. This is a long-term method that can generate amazing results, but it needs a lot of time and effort to do. By customizing your store products for specific keywords, you will make sure that you send the correct traffic from search engines to your site.

Similarly, creating quality and informative content will preserve old visitors and attract new customers. In terms of the return on investment, there are a few methods that create more benefits than a great SEO and content strategy.

Ads can only allow you to earn short-term benefits, because those who come to your site may not return again. But SEO will help you in the long run. Quality content will rank in search engines for months and even years since it was last published.

Again, there is one more important thing to understand: The average rate of conversion for e-commerce stores is around 2%. In other words, for every 1000 people who land on your site, 20 will purchase something from it. That also implies that if you are getting less than 100 visits to your site per day, you will hardly make any profit.

There are many ways to polish your conversion rates, and it needs an in-depth knowledge of marketing skills and tools. In the end, there are two primary goals: To get more visitors, and convince many of them to purchase.

7. Apply some classic sales tricks

If a person was to assist you with purchasing a camera for $300, you might not be that interested, even if you are searching for one. But throw in a great lens, a camera bag, and some SD cards, and the deal now looks sweeter.

With your dropshipping store, you can apply the tactics of large merchandisers and create attractive deals that your customers won't deny. If possible, develop bundles and sales to attract shoppers to give it a second look. Many people won't remain loyal to purchase, but change their mind with a product on sale.

8. Create your own dropshipping store

As you plan to put your entrepreneurship skills into reality, take time to create a functional, well-designed and profitable store. Let your store attract visits and sales.

We recommend Shopify for this matter.

In conclusion, regardless of the challenges that dropshipping comes with, many entrepreneurs still have their hopes on dropshipping because of the low startup costs involved. Also, those who have identified their niche industries become more familiar with the supply chain of their unique market and then start to dominate it. As a result, dropshipping can be considered as a challenging business that still has a great profit potential for those who are ready to learn and master the process.

Reducing shipping costs and mastering the supply-chain channel has helped most dropshippers make a profit in a tough e-commerce industry. Outsourcing your shipping model, for example, is something that has made dropshipping a viable business for generating passive income. One thing that is true is that, despite the complexity of the digital marketplace, shortcuts like dropshipping will continue to be used by clever entrepreneurs for many years to come.

Badass Passive Income Ideas That Your Teacher Won't Tell You

Chapter 27: Sell Music

The dream of any artist is to make a living from their music, but how do you start making money? First, you need to know that you don't need to have links or get lucky to create a fan base and grow your income as an artist.

As long as you are creating good music in a genre that has a great audience, there is an easy way to predictably and reliably expand your fan base while you concentrate on making the music. Music can be a great way to generate passive income.

Before you can learn how to generate passive income from music, it is important to look at mistakes that some artist make.

1. **Upload music and pray**

Many of us think that when we finish creating an album and send it to the worldwide network, the work is done.

We think that Bandcamp, CDBaby, and ReverbNation, or any other powerful distributor will do the heavy-lifting for us.

It is estimated that there are over 30,000,000 songs available for download, purchase, and streaming.

Thirty million!

That is more than the combined number of people in Rome, Paris, New York, and London.

So, when you upload your music to the worldwide distributor, the song gets lost in the giant sea of music. So the best way not to make anything from your music is to upload it and hope that, one day, it will get famous.

Well, uploading and hoping that the music will one day become a hit is a strategy that will not work.

2. Sign a record deal

This is like begging a company to listen to your songs. Unfortunately, this is still a popular method until now. Because musicians have been conditioned to think that once you sign a record deal, all your problems are solved and money starts to flow like water.

You say goodbye to struggling. It is all mansions, limousines, and fitness models.

Right?

Again, not like that.

The reality is that record deals are some of the worst ideas on planet Earth. In fact, they are more advantageous to the company.

Since the job of the record company is to make as much money as it can from your music, you will rarely rake the benefits of your music.

And there is isn't a huge advance payment you get. The money they fund you to set up the music, you will have to pay it back, keeping in mind that what you earn is very little. So it is easy to see how a huge percent of artists who sign a record deal end up owing money instead to their record label.

Another thing is that record companies have devised ways to add costs and charge artists. When a record company executive flies to see you perform, you shouldn't feel happy. But you need to be extremely upset.

Why?

That's because you are going to pay for all his costs, including the expensive jet and champagne. Everything is all on your tab… and nobody may even bother to ask for your permission to use your money.

By the time the record company removes all the expenses and add-ons, most artists only earn two pennies out of each dollar their music generates. So you need to create a solid plan on how you are going to manage your income when you decide to sell your music as a means to earn passive income.

Record companies don't sign deals with new up-coming artists… unless the artists have a huge growing fan base. It's a hard time for record companies because they only want to sign deals with artists who are already generating good income.

Well, if you are making money from selling your music, why in the world would you want to sign with a record company? And why in the world would you let them take 98 percent of your money from your songs and your performances?

3. Assume that Facebook will make you famous.

Say, you aren't going to sign a record deal, and you are also not going to upload music and hope that it will sell.

How are you going to market your music, then?

Well, you know the answer, dont you?

You will not make anything if your goal is to sit and think that Facebook will market your music for you.

In other words, you must up your marketing game and push your music, for it to be known all over the world. Social media is a great way for entertainment and developing one-on-one relationships with other humans. However, social media is terrible if you want to motivate people to buy anything. Depending on the market strategy you employ, social media will either break or destroy your music.

But you need to know that it's not going to be shiny. It's not new. It's not flashy. It's not sexy. So what is it?

That said, how can you make money from selling music?

Create a mailing list

This is what you need to do, and it is advised that you employ this strategy if you want to boost your passive income from selling music and growing your fan base.

It's basically a simple process:

Build an email list full of fans, and create a genuine relationship with them over time. Next, invite them to purchase your songs.

That's it.

It looks simple, right? We thought it has to be something cosmic. But cosmic isn't more effective.

Well, there could be millions of counter-arguments against this strategy.

"People don't read email…"

"People don't like email…"

Here's the thing, each of the above critiques has a specific merit.

Email is probably not perfect. But email is the most perfect method found to spread the word about your music and invite people to purchase.

Averagely, for each dollar spent on email marketing, the profit earned is $2.22.

That translates to 122 percent return on investment (ROI), for those who like to do the calculations.

And here's is something else you need to be aware of creating an email list and learning the way to communicate with PEOPLE on your list, but it takes time.

But that isn't a big deal. After all, no one learned to play a musical instrument on the first day. And neither did you learn how to sing in a day. So it's not bad that building a career takes some time.

Luckily, it is not that difficult.

The 3 steps to make money with your music:

It all narrows down to three simple steps.

First, you must locate fans of your genre.

Identify your fans

This is the point where social media comes in.

Some genres have a massive online community that you can join to become a member. Other genres may not, and you will have to search further to identify where fans hang out.

For some genres, the only sure way to link with fans online is through paid advertising. Don't be scared though – it's not as hard as it looks, and there is a simple process that you can use to dial things in. Once you know what you need to search for, it is very easy to make a profit.

Once you identify where most fans spend their time, you can then attract signups to your list.

Attract signups to your list

Yes, it is about building your list.

Besides your songs, your email list is the most valuable resource you have. But make sure you don't redirect people to Twitter, Instagram, Facebook or Snapchat, or anyplace else.

But you can send them to your landing page.

Here, you will provide them with a sample of your music and create for them an exclusive offer for some of your best work.

Set it as free in exchange for their email address.

Follow a proven strategy to sell your music

What is this proven strategy?

Easy.

Build friendship with your new subscribers.

Be real. Be genuine. Be honest. Be open. And show them a glimpse of your process.

Tell them real stories about you.

Don't disrespect them by sending them nonstop sales messages.

Offer them things that they will never get if they weren't on your list. Make them want to hear from you next.

If you can do these things, they will purchase your music even today, when they don't have to buy any songs from anyone. Your secret weapon is a genuine connection with your fans. This gives them a real experience about you.

Does this really work to expand your fan base?

If you are like most artists, you might be saying, "This can't work. Nobody wants more email."

Except that it works like charm.

Here's the reason why:

Nobody wants to receive a crappy email. However, everybody wants awesome things in their inbox. If you spend some time to do it right, you will be surprised at the response.

Just remember two things:

Create great music that fans will enjoy listening to.

Build an email list of fans and customers, and treat them like family and friends. They will support your career. Making money selling music should be a simple process. But it is necessary to remember two things:

First, you are not going to ball with Gulfstreams and Bentleys overnight. You are building a business and that will take time. There's a great learning curve, and everyone makes mistakes along the way. But if you hold it firmly until the end, you will be surprised at how far you can reach.

Secondly, just like recording, writing, and production, mastering your songs is vital.

There are some little things to master:

More simple ways to begin making passive income from your music

1. **Digital streaming revenue**

Digital streaming drives sales in the UK. Spotify pays an average of 0.00437p per stream. In other words, if you get 1 million streams, you will make over £4,000. This may not look like a huge amount of money, but Spotify is an easy means to gain exposure and open other opportunities for you to make money.

To start making money from Spotify, post your music to user-curated Spotify playlists, marketing your Spotify on social networks, and blogs. Over time, the Spotify algorithm will notice that your streams are increasing, that you are being added to playlists and similar bands to you.

With the Spotify submission tool that lets you send upcoming material to Spotify officials, marketing Spotify is easier to do by yourself. You could find yourself on the main playlist, creating a large number of streams in no time, which results in receiving payment.

Sometimes, people complain about royalties they earn from Spotify, but apart from paying a distributor to have it posted, the platform is free for your music to be on. You are being presented with a chance to make money on a free platform. This is a great opportunity that you cannot complain about.

2. **Perform live**

People love to listen to music. On the other side of the coin, artists love to play music. So it's a perfect match for the creator and consumer. Gigging is a profitable side income of the music industry, with industry estimates that live music can be raking in $31 billion worldwide in 2022.

The odds that you will be making money from the tickets sold online, and many other ways, are high. But there are also two other methods to make money from live events.

a) **Festivals**

Besides gigs, there are festivals that pay artists well. Festivals create the opportunity to play music alongside popular big brands, get music promotions and gather an audience, which may not be possible at a gig. All these generate a different income source.

b) **Live royalties**

You can easily begin to gather copyright royalties for performing. If you are registered to PRS and you perform a song that you have written and registered with PRS, they will pay you for the performance. Each venue has a PRS license to handle the costs of paying out these royalties, so ensure that you do your research and take advantage of this. Every little penny counts, so you shouldn't be afraid to ask your marketer about this.

3. Merchandise

Closely related to live performance is merchandise. If people come to your live shows, they are going to be fans who love your music and this means they are happy and proud to confess that they listen to your music. So they would also be proud to buy your merchandise. But they won't be proud to put on a poorly-designed, or a cheaply-designed t-shirt with just your brand name written on their chest.

Be creative your designs. Create a design that not only represents you as a musician, but also a design that people will want to wear even if they haven't listened to your music. At the end of the day, merchandise is something that you can make a large income from, so don't go cheap. If possible, look for a professional graphic designer to come on board. If you create something that is visually attractive, of good quality, and in general a strong product, you can even go ahead to charge more, and people will still invest in it.

4. YouTube Revenue

Some years ago, musicians who wanted to become popular would send their record to labels and sit and wait to be signed. But in the modern age, you can apply different creative approaches to get your music heard all over the world. This allows you to make money from loyal fans and listeners across the world. One place that this works perfectly is YouTube.

YouTube works with musicians from all over the world to create revenue and assist the musician to earn more. Artists who put post their music through third-party distributors can submit music to

YouTube and gather money from ads and YouTube premium. Also, distributors who use the YouTube Content ID system can gather revenue from other YouTube videos like Vlogger, who might use your music.

Another method to generate money through YouTube is to begin by creating content yourself, which can earn you some income. You don't necessarily make money based on the views you get – you generate the money based on the level of interaction of people with the ad shown before or during your video, which will definitely be higher if you have a lot of people seeing your videos.

For that reason, if you create high-quality content which involves a large audience, will begin to generate money for yourself. Easy methods to begin doing this as a musician is to organize tour diaries, and vlogging on a daily basis. Be creative with your content and you will get a loyal fan base, and soon an income will follow.

5. Brand Collaborations

If you have a large following, you are selling gigs, and you have just begun to make a solid income from your music, where can you look next to start making more income? Well, this is the time to approach brands and sponsors you want to work together with.

Start in your local area. Locate local brands that work well with your style, lifestyle, and image. Call people, send out emails, and DM some on Instagram offering them a deal that they cannot resist. Whether you are going to offer the brands social media posts that will grow their following or be wearing their merchandise, discuss with the brand to settle on a deal that works best for both parties.

6. Crowdfunding

This involves raising a certain amount of money from a large group of people. In the case of an artist, you request your fans to donate something small, with the end goal to collect something big. Your fans want to support you and your music career, so crowdfunding can be a superb way to gather money while networking and giving back to your fans.

But how do you do it? First, you must identify the platform on which you want to use to crowdfund. There is a lot to select from, but Patreon and Kickstarter have a good reputation. So you can start with them. You need to set a goal of how much you want to collect, plus the deadline. If you hit your goal on time, you will get all the money you managed to collect. But if you fail to fulfill your goals in time, every donation send by your fans is refunded. So, aim to be realistic so that you can make quick money. Convince your fans that you want to work together to produce something. Also, set a challenge that you can attain together.

One thing that you must consider is: Why should a fan send you money? If someone stopped you while walking in the street and requested for £3,000 to build their next EP, would you accept their offer? The response is probably a resounding no, and your fans will react the same way unless you are giving them something in return. So you need to be imaginative and work together with your fans to learn exactly what they want. Maybe anyone that sends over £100 wins a live session performed at their house. It is easy to create a crowdfunding page, but it is not easy to receive the donations, so you must show that you are working for it and that you appreciate every single penny that comes through.

7. Create value

Selling music isn't a big challenge for individual artists, but the problem is obscurity. Nobody wants to know who you are, so they won't pay for your music. But you need to look at your music as a marketing tool, instead of a means of income. If your whole business model for your music is to sell albums, your model is old-fashioned and unsuccessful. But you should try to make your music available to everyone, and then you can concentrate on generating value.

Take time to think about the future. If you charge people for music that they have never listened to, it will not be bought, but if you concentrate on building a loyal fan base, providing them with enough music as you can do, your product will soon rise in demand. This means that you can start to think about sales. If you create a valuable product, people will pay for it, and this works with the music you create.

Earning a solid income as a solo artist is easier than ever, with platforms ready to play your music and letting your fan base grow. Selling your music in ways that never existed before is now possible. In this internet era, the money lies in the audience you can get.

One last thing: Get started. Now!

Learning is great. But just as with music, it's all about doing. None of this information will help you if you don't take time to build a marketing system that will expand your fan base.

So, dive in, and you could be earning passively from your music videos.

Chapter 28: Sell Print-On-Demand Products

Have you ever wanted to become part of the e-commerce revolution and launch your passive income business?

Well, there are a lot of things to consider before you can get started. What do you want to sell? Where will you find your target customers? How are you going to market your store? What business model will you apply?

Opening a Print-On-Demand (POD) store is a viable way to generate passive income online. For most people, it's a way of living and is also easy to venture in because, for less than $100, you can get your first store running.

Are you interested? Let's dive deeper.

What is Print-on-demand?

Briefly, POD is an online business model where the production and shipping process of e-commerce products are outsourced. You sell products printed on "blanks" – bags, t-shirts, and other merchandise. You post images to your partner apps, and the products to your web store, and divide the profits of each sale.

When people purchase your product, the orders get printed, packaged and delivered by your printing partner. You pay the supplier for their work and materials. What you remain with is the profit.

Say you pay $9 for a t-shirt with your custom design already done. You list it on your e-commerce store for $25. Another person buys it;

your printing partner receives an order and completes it. You sold it for $25, paid $9 to the supplier and made $16.

It is that simple, right?

The best thing is that you only need to pay for what you have sold, which translates to little to no capital risk. Additionally, you don't need to be worried about your inventory shipping. You can concentrate on sales and expand your business. That is the best side of POD shipping.

Ups and Downs of Print-On-Demand Business

Of course, POD seems like a gold mine, but that isn't true. There are challenges and benefits to it that you should consider. Let's find out.

The Pros of POD

1. **You need low capital to start**: Unlike traditional retailers, you don't need to invest thousands of dollars into your idea before you even begin to sell. $100 is still enough to get started. You will get your domain name, Shopify subscription, or even a great WordPress theme with some premium plugins. You don't need to keep anything, but you will need to have a complete catalog.

2. **Easy to set up**: The time of hiring a web designer is over. With all themes at your disposal, plugins, guides, and templates, you can get your store up and running in no time.

3. **Easy to try out with product designs**: When you are aiming for something new, you will only need to organize it with your print partner and add it to your store.

4. **No need to have an inventory space**: Your supplier handles the rest while you concentrate on selling.

5. **You get access to external markets**: Your store will be able to ship goods anywhere your manufacturer can ship goods. And most manufacturers deliver products across the world.

6. **Scale and test** new products without any financial risk. You are able to see the type of designs that sell fast and which ones don't, so you can easily adjust.

7. **The ability to customize and sell** your special designs. If you are a graphic designer or someone who knows people that generate beautiful visual content, POD presents the chance to generate money by building up your own unique brand.

8. **Products are difficult to copy:** Unlike the dropshipping business, no one will have similar products as you do.

When you can sell unique products, you tend to create your own brand and repeat customers. This is advantageous in the long term.

The cons of POD

1. **You will need to look for a partner with quality "blanks":** Since you don't have any control over the production process, you need to look for a trustworthy supplier who maintains a high-quality production and fulfills all the order requirements all the time.

2. **There is a low entry barrier:** Even when you know you sell the best merchandise from the best designs, you still need to be strong. Your suppliers work together with your competitors, and there are many of them. The competition can be stiff, so bring in your creativity.

3. **Order fulfillment and reputation depend on your suppliers:** The logistics of your business can become a challenge as the business grows. If your supplier ships from

more than two warehouses, the problem can get worse – wrong addresses and shipping delays can add up to chase away a customer.

4. **Order fulfillment and delivery can take around 2 weeks:** In the worst case scenario, delays and mistakes will result in frustrated customers and thus negative reviews. Even the best customer service can do little about it.

5. **It takes patience to find a profitable niche and notice good designs:** Understanding the ins and outs of POD business takes time. It takes time to get a reliable supplier, it takes time to discover a profitable design, and it takes effort to grow your business.

6. **Returns can be a hard thing to handle:** So you should ensure that your return policy goes hand-in-hand with your supplier's.

7. **There could be some added costs:** If you are serious about your business, you may have to spend more to sell. Payment gateway, domain registration, plugins, and paid ads do cost more, but it also provides you with a competitive advantage.

As you can see, there are a lot of things to consider before you make a final decision to set up your POD store. But still, there is lower risk and hassle as compared to opening a normal e-commerce store. But you aren't in a hurry yet to make that decision.

First, let's show you how you can open your POD store that sells:

Starting a POD business that sells

By now, you are familiar with the concept behind a POD store.

Theoretically, it goes this way: You develop a website and find your original designs, get a suitable POD vendor and market your products till you make sales. The manufacturer prints your product, packages it and ships it to your customer. When the customer gets the goods, all parties involved win. Both you and the supplier make a profit and the customer gets what he or she wants.

Practically, it needs more work than that. You must know the type of products and niche to choose for your POD store.

1. Niche and products to select for your POD store.

You may decide to use mugs, t-shirts, phone cases, etc., as the raw products to place your designs. But you shouldn't make that decision before you conduct in-depth research. First, you must identify a niche that will allow you to thrive. It can be something specific like "cats on synthesizers in space" or a broad one like "manga comics." If you don't have a specific idea in mind, create a list of 20-30 things that you prefer. For example, ecotourism, basketball, biking, etc. The more specific you are, the easier it will be to stand out and identify your customers.

Once you have your list, start to validate ideas. You can switch to Facebook, Twitter, or Google Trends to find out what people are saying. If there are more active and passionate people talking about your subject, they could possibly be your potential customers.

Next, you can scale down your list to a few fundamental ideas with the best promise. Confirm with other social sites on what is being discussed. The more posts and discussions that are available, the better.

Lastly, navigate to Google, Amazon, or eBay and try to identify what has already been sold in your niche. Don't be scared if someone has discovered an idea which resembles yours. Pay attention to the number of reviews – that is a good sign that shows if those products definitely sell.

If you are a designer in your specific niche, then you don't have to reinvent the wheel. If you have an audience already, they are definitely going to love your new merchandise, too.

Once you identify an idea, you may also need to understand the kinds of products to sell. There are thousands of products to select from. For starters, you may want to hold on to what is popular. The most common POD products include mugs, t-shirts, notebooks, pillows, phone cases, and posters.

Despite the numerous choices, the focus here is to arrange your products in accordance to your market desires. Make sure that your designs are printed on products that make sense. But don't stress too much to make it look perfect – mistakes won't cost you much anyway, and there will be a lot of room for experimenting.

2. **Get your website and designs ready**

After you understand your niche and your major products, then the real task starts. If you don't have a website, it may appear overwhelming at first.

Getting your Print-On-Demand Designs

Finding cool designs is simple if you are a graphic designer or artist. You simply tell your talent what motivates you online in your style, and you will be on the correct track.

For everyone else, it may prove a bit troublesome. You cannot just steal the designs you like – it is prohibited. But, you can purchase them. Below are some great places where you can get your designs ready:

- Fiverr
- Upwork

- Design Pickle
- EComLibrary
- **DesignerCash**

Getting your Print-On-Demand Website Ready

Setting a website requires at least a few days, but it's worth your time. Keep in mind that it will be your home – sales center of marketing activities.

a) Sign up a domain name: You could even get one at GoDaddy or a different service provider. You are creating a brand around it, so you need to make it relevant to your niche, and easy to recall.

b) Select a platform for your website: Once your domain name is ready, it is time to prepare your web store. The easiest way to do this is to use:

- Etsy
- Shopify
- Wordpress + WooCommerce

c) Design your store

Shopify, Etsy, and WordPress provide easy customization templates. Get started with these sites as your starting point. You may need to go through all the basic pages, payment, and shipping information.

You may also want to add a premium theme or plugin to generate a better experience for yourself. Make your site easy and pleasant to navigate and buy products. For instance, a great idea is to install an abandoned-cart plugin that will email your customers a discount code if they leave the site without buying anything.

d) Donthey leave

Over time, a well set up store will pay for itself. So don't try to sell your products cheaply.

e) Supercharge your store with your partner Dropshipping plugin. Once your site is more or less ready, it is then time to select a print provider.

3. **Choose your print provider and place the products in your store**

When you use the Shopify Sourcing App, WooCommerce + Dropshipping add-ons, you can complete your website and convert it into a web store.

Remember that by selecting a POD plugin for your store, you will also be selecting a partner that will meet your orders.

A reliable print partner makes all the difference between successful and failed POD retailers – yes, that is critical!

4. **Market your Print-On-Demand store to optimize sales**

Marketing is an important part of every Print-On-Demand business. Without marketing, you will be like a book on a shelf in a large library. Nobody knows that you exist until someone accidentally meets you. You must simplify processes to get your business. How well you do it will be shown by the number of sales you achieve.

Chapter 29: Sell Software

With a rise in the popularity of computers, the idea of earning money selling software online can look like a great thing to do. If done in the right way, it can be an easy means to make money. This can also be an excellent passive-income-generation idea in particular, if you are marketing something that people really need.

However, being successful in this field is a bit more difficult than it first looks. There is a huge amount of competition that you need to consider. In addition, you need to think long and hard to determine what you want to create or market, to make sure that you make money. This chapter will look at some of the complexities involved in selling software, and how to go about it in the right way.

Sell your own software

If you are serious about selling software online, then one of the first things to decide is whether the software is your own, or whether you are going to make the software.

Of the two methods, creating your own software is definitely not easy. First, you must have a decent knowledge of the programming language in which you want to create your software. You also need to build something that will help people. In other words, this should be something that will solve a problem that people experience. Typically, this may mean that you create something unique, better than current existing software in the market.

This is doable, but you will have to sweat a little bit – sacrifice your time and money.

Even with the availability of all the softwares on the market, there are still fields which haven't been tapped into and problems whose solutions are yet to be found. If you can come up with an idea that falls into one of these categories, then the possibility of making a profit exists.

You need to remember that it can take a bit of time, however, to develop good software that would generate profit once you launch it. In addition, it will cost you money, especially if you decide to outsource some of the work. You might spend money and years to compile a piece of software, so make sure you do enough research beforehand to see whether there's a market for your product.

Now, you can cut down on your workload by beginning with something different, like purchasing something similar and making it even better. You can also use open-source software (OSS). But if you use similar software, make sure you read the restrictions. If not, you may dedicate your time and energy into improving something which you don't have any legal rights to sell.

Another similar sector to consider would be app development. Building useful apps, or even just games, can be significant even with simple ideas. Back in the year 2009, the iPhone Fart App was generating $10,000 per day. Still, games are making many sales, but building some niche apps could generate you a substantial passive income in the next five years.

Selling software developed by others

Building your own software product isn't easy, but a tough journey. The one advantage of selling your own software is that you can make more in sales as long as you didn't spend so much into the development phase.

If you are going to sell software created by a different person, the mathematics changes significantly:

For one thing, you must know, there is a minimum risk involved selling someone else's software. First, you didn't pay anyone to develop the software, so you lose less if the software doesn't sell. Instead, you can decide to shift to a different product if you discover that the first type of software doesn't sell as well as you thought.

You can even decide to sell more than one software at the same time. This includes software from competing companies. This increases your odds of success because you are dealing with a variety of software products. Create a comparison of different anti-virus programs, and highlight the pros and cons – and boom, you generate sales from all the companies selling anti-virus softwares, when all you did was compile the information.

You may also find software that has a great reputation. So, some people may have heard about it, and even used it at some point in their life. In this case, what you are trying to sell is already familiar with a good number of people, including the company. Therefore, the reputation implies that you are likely to sell more software that already exists than something that you make yourself. In most cases, people may only be looking to confirm that they don't get scammed and that they are getting the right product for their needs – and their needs would be fulfilled.

Well, how do you earn credit for sales with affiliate links?

When it comes to affiliate marketing, you will not be literally selling the product, but you will be playing the role of a salesperson. This means you will be directing people to the software and market it. In other words, you are the intermediary with all the information to market it. Someone is searching for information, and your website has all the information and links to the vendor's website page. When the buyer goes on to click your link, you receive credit.

The link has your affiliate code and drops a cookie.

For instance, you may do a review to show people how well it works and what you should expect from it. You can create a written review, or a video review, or even both. You can attach screenshots, opinions, and technical stats. This is very useful to consumers, as people are looking for information about how the product works before they can move forward to purchase.

Similarly, you could manage to persuade people about the software they haven't even heard of. They may look for a product that has been hyped, but you feel isn't worth the money. You can then send them to a better or even cheaper option. For instance, someone may want to edit images and think they need Photoshop. However, that is billed at $20 per month, and only the pros need it. For simple image edits, you can go for SnagIt or Pixelmator which requires only a one-time fee, and is much easier to use.

This is just an example, but you can market SnagIt through affiliate marketing and generate a commission every time someone purchases it. In fact, you can market anything that has an affiliate network. Even if your site does most of the photo editing, you can also make money by suggesting related hardware.

Creating your own affiliate site

Affiliate marketing is a great tool. You don't even need to own your products or build anything to generate money, so it becomes easy to scale up your profits. Informational articles you create will remain online forever. Therefore, a post that generates 2 sales per day can make you 2 sales a day for the rest of your life.

Some people decide to do affiliate marketing through forums, or social media. Thus, they post recommendations along with their affiliate link wherever they can. In the short run, this may work, but it isn't a great long-term plan. In most cases, posting affiliate links in social places will result in your account being banned.

If you create your own site and do affiliate marketing via it, then you have a percentage of internet real estate that you can grow as time goes by. As you develop the site, you will build more content, which will assist you to rank in search engines. As time goes, you build your own reputation via links and social shares. This will allow you to get more traffic and boost your likelihood of sales. You are also building a valuable resource – something that people may revisit at different times.

When you develop your website, one of the most critical things is the topic, which is referred to as a "niche". If your niche is internet marketing, you may decide to market software that will assist people to make money online. In the flipside, if your niche is low-carb cooking, you can market software that will allow people to know the number of carbs in a specific meal and compute their total carbs intake for the day.

Other interesting topics to focus on include antivirus software, stock trading software, home video monitoring systems, and bookkeeping software.

In general, you will customize the specific software you are marketing around, and what your audience is going to be interested in. Not many people search for "software" in general, and so you will need to be specific to catch the attention of an audience.

The one thing to say about affiliate marketing using your own website is that this industry is a bit easy to get started in. You don't need to invest a lot of money because the only necessary costs are a domain name and hosting.

If you want to start your own affiliate site, it is important to go get some training. The best place to find the right training is the Wealthy Affiliate. The training offered here is one of the best, in that you will learn everything.

They don't have attractive ads like "make money online" products do, and won't give you a false promise. You will have to work to expand your site. But they have a plan that works.

Make money as a software reseller

This is yet another profession that will earn you some money. While the previous method involves working as an affiliate, as a software reseller, your responsibility is to purchase software at a wholesale price and then sell it higher to make some profit.

As a software reseller, you can work alone or together with the company. They purchase from wholesale vendors, or sometimes directly from the manufacturer. Then, they sell the products directly to the end users.

Reselling software can be a very interesting business. However, it can be more difficult compared to selling hardware devices.

Reseller vs. Distributor

When you are searching online for information about software reselling, some information will also pop up about working as a software distributor. Well, if you are wondering whether there is a difference between these two terms, the short answer is yes.

Some basic differences between resellers and distributors include:

- Distributors have a close link with customers

- Distributors can provide services associated with branding, marketing, and labeling

- Distributors take the inventory of a product, while resellers do not

- Resellers often act strictly as an intermediary between customers and manufacturers

Since there is some risk to manufacturers, resellers tend to do work with established product lines or companies.

Methods to use to resell software

There are different methods that a software programmer or developer can work with a reseller to boost their sales. Some of the most common methods include:

- Re-branding
- Customizing the software for every customer
- Reselling software as is, plus the original branding and resale license

Some developers still build affiliate programs as part of the resale process.

The amount of money that resellers pay for the software depends on the type of package.

If they are going to sell a low-priced online package, they could just make a single payment for the software and resale rights. However, sometimes they pay a specific percentage per sale or size of the royalties from the software.

How can you get started?

The step to get started as a software reseller is a bit more complicated than just buying and selling. There are specific legal conditions that you need to fulfill. Follow these procedures to make sure you are ready to do business as a software reseller:

File for an EIN

Some resellers will not want to use their Social Security number to carry out their businesses.

In the following case, the first thing that should be done is to get in touch with the Internal Revenue Service (IRS) and file for an Employer Identification Number (EIN).

Register for a Reseller License

Depending on the laws of your state, you may want to sign up for a reseller certificate. Besides sharing information about yourself, you will also need to verify what you are reselling and how you plan to resell it.

Conduct your research

You have acquired an EIN and license, so you are set to start reselling software. Begin by getting in touch with companies that sell to resellers at an affordable price.

You will have to scale down the type of software you are interested in reselling, then make a comparison to identify the type of company that will give you the best price.

Contact developers

Once you know the type of companies that you want to work with, contact them and present your reseller's certificate. This will assist you to avoid paying sales tax.

Begin to sell

After this, you need to be ready to purchase the software and begin selling, either from your store or website.

Keep in mind to collect sales tax from the people who buy the software. But you don't need to collect sales tax from a buyer outside your state.

Pay taxes

Don't forget your tax mandates.

Resellers are just like other business people – they need to submit quarterly collected sales tax to the department of revenue.

To simplify the process, make sure you keep accurate records of all your sales.

Ensure you monitor your sales and payments received on a spreadsheet.

Don't forget that companies such as eBay and Amazon report sales numbers to the IRS once it surpasses a certain target. Remember to pay taxes on any sales you generate through the platform. You will be in a big problem with the IRS if you don't.

Bonus tips

These tips will assist you to start well and ensure you succeed as a software reseller:

Apply your expertise

You probably participated in software reselling because you understand something about software development and programming. Utilize this knowledge to generate sales.

You may also market yourself by helping customers prepare their new software, or set up changes to customize it.

These types of services reduce the workload of the developer and increase the odds to keep working with you.

Good customer service

Good customer service is important, regardless of what you are selling.

Some practices that will set you apart from other resellers include:

- Fast responses to emails, or calls before and after the sale.

- Offering accurate descriptions of your products.
- Developing a clearly stated and fair return policy.

Certain resellers also provide complete refunds for malfunctioned products, plus an extra percentage for the inconvenience of having to return it.

This may appear as a disservice to you, but the reality is that it will improve your customer service ratings and result in higher profits.

Chapter 30: Sell Stock Photos

Whether you are a professional photographer looking for new methods to earn income, or interested to find new means for a side income, selling stock photographs can be an important tool.

While there are a lot of ways you can earn a living from photography, selling stock photography is always overlooked, although it is unlikely to generate a full-time income from it. Still, it can be a great way to make some extra cash to supplement your monthly income.

What is stock photography?

To help you understand stock photography, assume someone on Facebook has contacted you. They want to purchase one of your photos posted online. You agree to the sale, then they send you money via PayPal and you provide them with written permission to use your photo.

What you have just done is to license one of your images as a stock photo.

That, in brief, is the way a stock photo business operates. In other words, it is licensing of existing photographs by another entity that will use it for a certain purpose. You develop the photographs and offer them for purchase. Then, a buyer licenses them.

Photographers who excel in this business usually take time to plan and do their research well on what type of photographs to create. Just taking random shots of pretty objects will not earn you even a penny.

The photographers who earn the most often work on it as a business. They come together and carefully plan what, where, and how they will shoot their subjects. They shall have researched markets and analyzed the current trends. In addition, they use props, models and authentic locations for their shots.

Where to begin

There is a high chance that you are already taking shots of things you love. Well, is your favorite topic suitable for stock photography?

You can consider stock photos as a product that must fulfill the needs of businesses. Your best subjects will determine the amount of profit you make.

Start by asking yourself: What is it that I love to take photos of? Who purchases what I love to take a photo of? How will I sell my stock photos?

Shooting ideas

Building images that are in demand involves research and planning. Stock photos that sell well make it because they demonstrate an idea.

The goal of a buyer is to find a stock image that fulfills a communication problem. This is often about a particular idea. There are over thousands of ideas that photo buyers look for and some include:

- Work
- Trust
- Quality
- Family
- Teamwork
- Reliability

- Performance
- Pride

Planning your photography session with ideas in mind will increase the market for your photos. Don't forget to acquire model and property releases from all private property and persons in your photography. That will eliminate any possibility of a lawsuit. As a result, you can reduce expenses.

Preparing to shoot

Most niches have a market, and the task is to identify them. If your passion lies in tropical birds, you can probably subscribe to publications dedicated to them. You can and will likely market to them.

Technical perfection is still important for selling better images. This involves quality lighting, pleasing compositions, perfect exposure, and subjects that look natural instead of posed.

In addition, the bestselling photos are well-styled with current trends and technologies. This can include clothing trends to the latest modern smartphone.

What should you shoot?

If you like to take shots of different subjects, remember that the subject is important. Business and technology plus lifestyle subjects are normally sold a lot. However, the demand for nature and wildlife is quite low.

If you are a landscape photographer and you plan to take shots of aviation because you think they are in demand, you need to get busy to become an excellent aviation photographer. Your competitors in this niche may have many years of experience, and that may not be easy for you to make it.

Lifestyle

Lifestyle images are a great subject. Some of the ideas in this category may include couples heading to the beach, cooking together, or even enjoying their children. Teenagers enjoying technology, hanging out with friends, dating, or on college campuses are very good markets.

Anything associated with financial security, early retirement, or living healthy, has an amazing market.

Business and industry

Don't ignore business and industry subjects. Technology is dynamic – it changes daily. As such, the use of the latest technology is in demand.

People at business meetings, high-tech scenes, manufacturing process, and employees working together are still marketable subjects.

When taking industry shots, make sure you look at other angles such as businesses that go green, reforestation, clean air, global warming, and wind power. These are areas that are currently in demand.

Outdoor photography

For outdoor photographers, there are a lot of markets to shoot for. There is a magazine that features every type of recreational sport and interests.

Manufacturers of outdoor products involve outdoor images in their marketing and advertising efforts. Non-outdoor related businesses use recreation and sports images.

Landscapes and nature are one of the most popular fields among photographers. However, when it comes to selling landscape stock photos, this field is challenging. It's a crowded niche and there are a lot of such images in the market. However, these photos are still being used in calendars, books, and magazines.

The marketable sections for stock photographers are limitless. Your strength and interests should determine what you shoot.

Beyond the capture

To successfully sell stock photos, you must be organized and efficiently run the business. After the photoshoot, the digital files have to be edited.

While you can choose to keep all your files, it is good to select only the best and market them. Maintain a horizontal and vertical version, look for sharpness and edit the file for the best quality.

Then, start to market only one version and when a buyer wants to see other versions, show them what you have in your store. However, you must learn to be ruthless with your editing so that you can only have the best.

If you doubt a photo, then it is better to throw it out.

You also need to have an organized image file. Great programs created to do this include Portfolio, Capture One, and Extensis. Each of the listed programs offers something unique. Your goal should be to identify the effective system for monitoring your images and cataloging.

Over time, the number of photos in your library will increase. Monitoring things such as image data and sales information is important. Should a client ask you about an image, you can then provide all the details they need.

Become an illusionist

Most photographers use Photoshop. And this can offer creative opportunities for stock photographers. Apart from making RAW files "usable", now it is possible to create photographs digitally. If you can picture this, then you should be able to create images in Photoshop.

A good place to start is on an idea that you want to do. Once you have taken the shots, you can digitally collect them to build more marketable stock photography.

Marketing and selling stock photos

If you don't have a customer ready to pay you to use your stock photos, they add no value. Getting your work in front of buyers can be difficult.

But there are two methods that you can achieve this: Becoming a member of a stock photo agency to sell your photos or by selling them yourself. Many photographers end up doing both.

Stock photo agencies require photographers to generate the best photos. The plus side of a stock agency is that they handle everything right from hosting to marketing, but at a given cost. The agents acquire a certain percentage of each sale, and that percentage relies on the agency.

Before looking for a photo agency, assess your library of unique photos. Agents will want what you have photographed in the past. But still, they are interested in what you will photograph in the future.

If you take similar photos of what everybody else does, then they may not accept you. But if you are taking shots in new subjects, they may be more interested to work with you. In short, you need to be creative in what you do.

Self-promotion

If you are going to sell your own shots, then you need to create a solid marketing strategy to get in touch with potential buyers. This is a bit easier when you market locally. Local photo buyers will comprise of marketing agencies, magazine publishers, graphic designers, and web design firms.

You can get them through online directories or phone books. Getting national addresses is more challenging, because of the large coverage with many cities and publishers.

Next, you have to decide whether you are going to market via email or print. There are many opinions about this, but email is much cheaper and affordable than printing direct-mail promotional pieces. The main challenge to email is the spam folder.

You don't know how many reached the client, and how many went into the spam folder.

How long can it take to make money with stock photography?

Stock photography can a bit frustrating if you take part in it with a short-term goal.

If you think you can use images from your last vacation and make some couple of hundred bucks by the end of the month, you may end up surprised. You may end up making zero profit. Even worse, your images may end up being rejected for technical issues.

The first thing about stock images is that they have to be good in all spheres. Even before you start to send a photo to a microstock website, you have a check that your images are of good quality.

You cannot expect to make money selling photos that have incorrect exposure settings, or have been edited incorrectly.

Think long-term if you are seriously interested in generating money selling the stock photos. There are many aspects that you need to factor in.

While some photographers on the internet think that stock photographs don't make sales, this is wrong even though you have a lot of competition to ward off. Despite the competition, you need to focus on the positive side. With the rise of the internet, there is a large market for stock photos.

With the rise and acceptance of microstock websites as a great resource for licensing images, business executives, part-time photographers, engineers and anyone else has at least a second means of earning income.

Slowly develop your portfolio, and you are likely going to get a great experience. The secret to succeeding in selling stock photographs is to develop that discipline, consistent approach, and significant research to boost your efforts.

Don't forget that with stock photography, the more images that feature in your portfolio, the higher amount of money you can possibly make over time.

Stock photography resembles the snowball effect.

Soon you will realize that your business starts to fund itself. If you take a look at stock photographers who have made it in life, they have thousands of photos in their portfolio. It is the effect of many years of persistent hard work without giving up.

However, there are some drawbacks too.

It is not new to hear that photographers have left a scene totally frustrated at how slow sales are and how little they make per month.

When you begin to sell stock photos, think big. But don't be over excited that you are going to make huge financial profits during the first few months. Expect to dedicate years of contribution to microstock sites so that you can expect a big financial reward.

Well, how much money can you make then?

This question depends on a few things:

- The number of photos you have in your portfolio
- The level of seriousness you put in stock photography
- How well-researched your subjects are, and how closely they define the demands of the client
- How well key-worded your photos are.

Some photographers use this channel as a means to supplement their source of income. Others turn this into their main form of income.

If you want to shoot stock, be confident and trust in your abilities. It will probably be helpful if you have the correct gear and the right post-processing tools.

Chapter 31: Sell WordPress Themes

There are many different ways you can make money with WordPress (WP). Have you ever thought of making passive income using WordPress? One of the best ways to earn a living using WordPress is by selling themes, and this chapter will teach you exactly how you can achieve that.

If you have used WordPress before, then you know that you can't run a blog or website without installing at least one WordPress theme or plugin. WordPress themes or plugins provide you with extra features so that you can run your blog successfully.

One of the main advantages of WordPress is the number of plugins and themes available – you can even use free themes and plugins. If you have the skills, you can build a theme to solve a particular problem within WordPress.

If not, you can build themes or plugins that your audience may find interesting to purchase. If you are planning to sell WordPress themes, you have to ensure that you concentrate on your audiences' need. This way, you will have a lot of opportunities to sell your newly created theme.

Sell premium themes

To make a living from selling WordPress themes, you need to develop two versions – free and premium. Once you have developed a premium theme, you can move forward to sell it in different ways such as from a website or from marketplaces. Whichever way you choose, each one has its own ups and downs.

Sell through your website

If you choose to sell a theme via your website, the greatest advantage is that you have total control over your income. This means you can control 100% of your profit. You can also build an attractive landing page on your site to allow visitors to discover your new WordPress theme, and then redirect them to the cart page.

The drawback of doing this, though, is that you will need to work on your site's search engine optimization (SEO). You need a great SEO so you can defeat your competitors and allow your audience to find your place.

Sell through marketplaces

When it comes to selling via marketplaces, you can have the biggest advantage of the exposure. Marketplaces have a large client base, plus a seamless payment system. If you are going to sell through marketplaces, you don't need to worry about getting buyers to visit your site.

Of course, there is also a problem if you choose to sell via a marketplace. One of the biggest challenges is that your profit is reduced. The marketplace receives a commission for every sale you make, but they help you gain exposure by letting you use their platform.

Sell on both

Another method is to sell your new WordPress themes both on your website and market platform. Your theme will stay on a WordPress repository, and when customers see it, you need a landing page where they will be taken to your website.

By placing your theme on market platforms, you will get immediate access to specific customers. This is one of the things that new WordPress sellers don't often know. With this particular approach, you can access both the pros and cons of each method so that you can earn more.

The best marketplaces to sell your themes

If you are searching for the best marketplaces to sell your WordPress themes or plugins, below is a list of some of the top places to go:

- **Themeforest:** This is a solid WordPress theme platform where new WordPress developers receive about 50% of their sales, and if they sell more, they can earn about 70% commission.

- **WP Eden:** This a new platform, but still one of the best marketplaces to sell themes. It permits the selling of themes and plugins with the potential to earn more than 75% commission.

- **Mojo Themes:** It is the fastest growing marketplaces for WordPress themes. It provides a commission of 50% to new developers and 70% to those developers that sell more.

Affiliate links

Affiliate networks are one of the fewer know strategies to make a living using WordPress themes. With this particular approach, you make use of services that easily reward you with commission for each plugin or theme sold.

There are different ways to sell your theme than the ones discussed here, but none is better than the other one. Instead, consider your current situation and determine the type of strategy that will best suit you. Give it a try, and if it works, then that is great. If it fails to work, then shift to another method until you find the best one for you.

Tips to help you build and sell a premium WordPress theme

Selling premium WP themes have become very popular among developers. This section offers you tips to consider when building and marketing WP themes.

A great company that has managed to market their premium themes to a particular niche is the Graph Paper Press. This company creates premium WP themes for photographers.

Adhere to the basic coding standards

When developing themes – in particular, themes that other developers may at one-point use, you should try and follow the basic WordPress coding standard. WordPress releases two types of coding standards, one for HTML and PHP, and the other for CSS. You can go and check detailed standards on their site.

You need to adhere to these standards because it will make it easy for other developers to follow and edit your code when they want to make some changes. Also, the marketplace expects you to adhere to a specific level of standards.

Before you publish your theme, you might want to try out a plugin that will test your code against the basic WordPress standards.

Be responsive with your design

Nowadays, it is important to develop a responsive theme. Most of the WordPress themes nowadays are responsive. If you want to sell your WP themes to a big percentage of buyers, then you should ensure that your theme is responsive. The good thing with a responsive theme is that it can work on different screen sizes.

This also works if you want your theme to stand out in the market. Some buyers simply pass a theme once they discover that it is unresponsive. Take time and use your creativity to build something which your buyers will enjoy.

Include the correct theme templates

WordPress has template guidelines of how themes should be named and how they should work on default pages and posts. With a premium theme, you need to assume that some users will want something basic to start with.

You will also have to include a custom template that is unique to a given design. Make sure you learn how to use the get_template_part() function, plus the naming conventions that come along with it.

Some themes – in particular frameworks, extend further by scaling up a theme into multiple ones to include files. Try to balance your theme to be flexible.

Research and select a niche for your theme

Usually, people will look for a premium theme that is customized to the content and purpose of the site they will use it for. Niches exist in different categories. Just to mention some of the niche themes that you should expect to find in WP include:

- Portfolios
- Non-profits
- Musicians
- Personal portfolios
- And many more.

By researching well on a niche, it will help you figure out what competition you should expect, and the odds of you making it in the market. When you finally select your niche for your particular theme, you will get a target audience you can market to. In addition, you can tell the type of keywords and marketing strategy that will work best for your theme.

Make your theme look attractive and amazing

Keep in mind that you aren't the only one selling WP themes in the market. In fact, there are thousands of WP-theme sellers on the market. If you want to stand out from the crowd as soon as someone sees it, then you must make your theme look amazing. You have to dedicate more time to the design of your theme.

This is not to forget the graphic elements, but also the type of content you include in the demo. Make sure that you use compelling images to display your theme's visual potential.

You might also want to involve numerous design options like color schemes, or even multiple page layout options.

Let your theme be easy to customize

You can easily know how much effort the developer has put into a theme in making it easy to customize when you work with a theme. You need to create some balance between providing many customization options and failing to include enough.

A complex theme can be frustrating to users. Two things that you need to do to help with this is to build an excellent theme options page and attach detailed documentation. Include different short codes and custom template which can make your site easy to customize.

You should hire some developers with different skills to help you set up and customize your theme before starting to sell it.

Create a comprehensive documentation

Good documentation should contain how to set up and configure a theme, plus how to use some of the custom templates you may have included. There is nothing more frustrating than buying a premium theme and not being able to change certain settings.

You can read more about the art of writing good WP documentation, and even download a documentation template to assist you to get started.

Most themes found in the marketplaces need you to include great documentation.

Make arrangements on how you will deal with support

Posting free themes on WordPress.org makes it easy to offer support because WordPress has an in-built support system for you to use. Some market platforms like ThemeForest, also have in-built support systems.

If you are developing your own website for your theme, then you will likely want to have a support system in place when you publish your theme.

You may also need to account for how much time you will spend to respond to threads and feature requests if your theme becomes popular. People who purchase premium themes expect that they will get rapid and instant help. You don't want to get featured as a theme developer with poor customer support.

Develop an interesting theme options page

A theme options page makes it possible for site administrators to edit specific features on the site without having knowledge of CSS or PHP. Many premium themes come with an in-built theme option that has different pages.

When you create a theme options page, ensure that you include things that people will use, and test everything before you release it.

If you adhere to every suggestion noted here, you will be well on your way to being a successful theme developer. Whether you want to sell multiple themes as a passive income or you want to develop themes, the abovementioned tips will be useful.

Chapter 32: Start a Vending Machine Business

Vending machines aren't a novel business idea, even though they are everywhere. When looking at the vending industry, you start to see how interesting it can be to set up a vending machine business. Take the USA, for example – there are more than five million machines. This means that this business makes billions of dollars per year as revenue.

The vending industry can be an attractive passive income stream for both new and experienced entrepreneurs. Besides the huge profits generated, the idea of launching a vending machine business may come to you because you saw a perfect location, have a great connection to vending-friendly items, or you know a person selling vending machines.

Whichever reason brought you to the world of vending machines, if you are looking for an alternative passive income stream, a simple way to expand your portfolio, or a low-cost startup business venture, then this could be the right business to do. With the perfect location, a great product selection, and user-friendly interface, a vending machine can consistently generate between $600-$800 in monthly revenue.

Are you ready to generate your fortune off grab-and-go snacks? Below is everything you need to know before starting a vending machine venture:

With just a few thousand bucks to invest, a vehicle, and you believe that you are ready to start a vending machine business and make it successful. However, just like any other business, starting a vending machine business isn't that easy, though you can inject fun and games into kick-starting your machine business. There is some preliminary financial planning and logistics involved.

Even before you can begin to research vending machines or read product reviews, assess the stock of your current finances. How much are you able to invest? Do not forget that it can take a year, even, for a machine to start generating profit. Once you know the amount of money you want to invest in the business, you are better equipped to begin looking for the best small-business financing.

And for entrepreneurs getting started in the vending business, figure out how you want to get into your local market by visiting public places with vending machines and retailers. Are you dealing with health foods, or are you looking to deliver standard snack and beverage services? Responding to these questions - even if your plans change later - will assist you to determine your location and type of equipment needed.

Lastly, be realistic with the expectations you set about profits and expenses. Owning and running a vending machine involves a low upfront capital, but you will need to dedicate time and energy into servicing, stocking and collecting money from your vending machines on a daily basis.

The Steps to starting a profitable vending machine business

Any insight you gather about a vending machine is a great way to get started on this particular niche. For instance, if you have identified a need for a snack machine around your place, get in touch with property owners you are aware of and figure out their interest in putting vending machines around their locations.

But still, without personal networks, you can begin a vending machine business and make money doing it:

1. **Determine your available options for a machine**

There are many more options available than a standard snack-and-soda machine. Most importantly, you should consider getting three types of vending machines, and select the machine whose products would be purchased by your target audience.

Regardless of the type of vending machine you select, you should get started with 1-2 machines with a defined market focus. This way, you can slowly learn about popular stock and site patterns, and add machines gradually.

2. Select the correct location for your vending machine

The make of the vending machine you purchase is important, but the place where you are going to install the machine is the most critical factor that will determine how much you profit you make. For example, an upscale machine may fail to generate good profit in a mall with a restaurant. However, the same machine may generate huge profits in an office park.

So the location where you choose to place your vending machine is very important, but you can always start with the first places you thought of while thinking about the idea of a vending machine. Additionally, consider the time you are likely to take to buy a beverage or a snack.

Other location ideas that you can consider include:

- Grocery stores
- Laundromats
- Apartment complexes
- Medical centers and hospitals
- Manufacturing plants

The next thing is to secure the location. A good salesperson can choose to cold-call the property owner or persuade them in person. This technique can work well for smaller locations in particular, if you already know the property owner.

You can still visit your local Chamber of Commerce – this will offer you comprehensive information about popular businesses around your area. This can also give you some ideas for possible locations. In general, try to install the machine around companies that have more than one hundred employees.

If you already have a place in mind, get in touch with proprietors, or aim to get contact information from the right manager. Speaking to prospective partners concerning the location requirements can assist you to get a better knowledge of local demand, and reveal your machine and product selection.

3. Get your machine

To identify your vending machine is as simple as doing online research. To get insights into different types and prices, look for both local and international suppliers. You need to also pay attention to the cost of inventory when searching for machine prices. You can start with the following outlets to get a vending machine of your dreams:

- Wholesale vending suppliers
- Consumer-to-consumer platforms such as eBay
- Secondary markets that allow you to search for multiple brands and machine models

As you conduct your online search, you will discover that the vending machine has different prices because of the various features. Some of those features include:

- Credit card and huge bill functionality
- Interactive screens
- Voice accessibility
- Remote monitoring software
- Drink-combination machines

Don't be deceived with these features, though. Still, they can be expensive – go for a machine that suits the products you want to provide, and what you can afford.

4. **Stock it with inventory**

Once you have gotten the machine, you have to stock it with the matching products.

Product selection is key to improving your sales. Instead of going for stock products based on popular foods and beverage, focus on local, site-specific needs. To be on the safe side, don't over-order stock at the start, and adjust what you will offer depending on the demand.

If you decide to offer a mixture of food and beverage services, drinks will be the highest percentage of your sales. The shape of drinks and their size will determine the type of your machine, so if you plan to sell irregularly shaped products, look for a machine with adjustable product sizes.

The vending machine business generates billions of dollars around the world every year. Fortunately, you can get into this attractive market with less than $1,000 with the right market, correct decision, and entrepreneurial energy.

Continue to invest as you learn more about the vending machine demand patterns, and begin generating passive income without the need for taking a huge loan. Depending on the situation, increasing the scope of your business slowly will create the opportunity to take on more when you are ready.

Whether you are financially stable or struggling, the vending sector offers an opportunity to run your own passive income stream while risking only as much as you are willing.

Chapter 33: Buying Patents and Licensing

If you had a great idea worthy of an investment and you spent months to brainstorm it, and now you have a patent for that idea, the next thing is to think of how you can make money from it. Filing for a patent isn't that cheap – that is the reason why you need to figure out how you can make money from it.

The value of your invention rests with you. Below are ways in which you can passively earn from your patents.

1. **Launch a business**

This is one of the best ways you can make money from your patent. Develop a business and start selling the product you created. If you are considering retail opportunities and manufacturing, ask yourself the following questions:

- Does your idea solve a real-world problem?
- Have you done some research to see whether consumers will like it?
- Does the idea result in a product that does better than the current products?
- Do you have the capital to market and produce the product?
- Can you manage to sell it at a competitive price?

Remember, building a business and selling a product are two different things that need different skills.

There are a lot of independent inventors that have decided to take the path of entrepreneurship.

When it comes to starting a business, you need to first have a business strategy. This is required by investors and bank lenders. But still, even if you don't need external funding to get started, it is important to have a business plan that outlines everything you need to do and accomplish.

2. License your patent

If you think launching your own business isn't the best way to go, you can still make some good income by licensing your patent.

Patent licensing is a strategy that allows you to transfer your patent rights to another entity that can use it to create a product or service.

Two types of patent licensing

- **Non-exclusive licensing** – The owner of the patent can generate the invention plus the license.
- **Exclusive licensing** – In this method, the owner of the patent will transfer all the ownership rights.

The advantages of licensing your patent

- Lack of capital will not prevent your idea from reaching the market.
- The trust and brand value of the license can build a legacy for you.
- Your invention sees the light in the form of a product.
- Your license can sell your product faster than you would.

However, patent licensing has its own ups and downs, so you need to read more about it before taking this route.

3. Involve a patent-licensing company

If you don't want to do all the licensing work yourself, you can involve companies such as Acacia Research Corporation. This company assists individual inventors to earn money from their patent assets. Typically, these companies work as middlemen – they link an inventor with a company that may help them with capital.

4. Use the patent as collateral in the bank

Sometimes, when you want to get a loan from the bank, you can use your patent as collateral. You could be surprised that that is a common practice and something that even major players like Kodak, General Motors, and Alcatel Lucent have done.

If a bank agrees that you can use your patent, it means that they recognize that your patent has significant value. This can really be a positive sign for companies wanting to acquire patents.

5. Sell your patent rights

Let's say you are not interested in licensing your patent – maybe the market for your intellectual property has started to vanish. It could be time to sell the patent.

Before you make that decision to sell your patent, ensure you ask yourself the following questions:

- Is there a method to expand your invention that may give your intellectual property more worth?
- Are you running out of methods to make licensing generate returns?
- Can patent pooling be possible?
- Where are you going to sell it?

6. Sell to a business that is growing in your country

Some patent owners decide to research and stay updated about overseas companies that are taking their operations to the international level.

Patents are location-based. In other words, you will require a patent for every country where you want to protect your idea. Therefore, when a company expands its activities to a new country, it will always try to get patents in the new country to prevent the possibility of being sued for infringement.

Normally, growing companies like to look for individual patent owners who are ready to sell.

In conclusion, to get a patent isn't a walk in the park as many may think. In fact, it is a complex, slow process, and expensive to boot. Just ensure that your patent generates a financial reward, regardless of whether you use it to create a product, or you license it to someone else. Don't just let your patent idle around. Let it generate passive income for you.

Conclusion

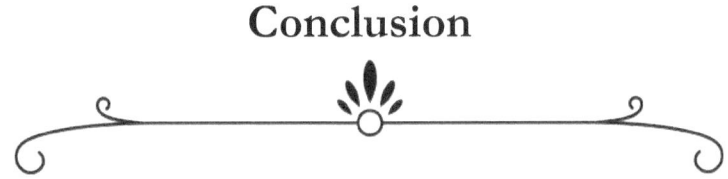

Passive income is real, but needs dedication and upfront work to make it a reality.

In addition, you will need to be patient because it can take some years before you can build a solid passive income base. The different options of passive income indicate that some will be more suitable for you than others.

Some means of passive income can be explored with a low capital while others may need a lot of capital. The good news is that the different streams of passive income exist and there is something there for everyone, at least. The secret is to get started, do enough research and see how it works for you.

Make sure that you start small and concentrate on increasing the size of passive income to become active income you generate over time.

As you can see from this book, there is a ton of ways to generate passive income. Hopefully, this entire list will help you scale down to a specific source of income that is right for you.

If you are tired of the traditional means of generating money, look for a few of the passive income streams discussed here so you can begin to work less and make more money. Keep in mind that persistence and hard work will pay off no matter what challenges you experience.

Other methods of making passive income include:

- Renting out a luxury bag
- Sell fonts

- Sell simple games
- Sell your own course
- Stream on twitch
- Writing quality articles on Medium.com
- Perform translation work for royalties

Good luck to you and we hope you gain financial freedom soon!

Connect with us on our Facebook page www.facebook.com/bluesourceandfriends and stay tuned to our latest book promotions and free giveaways.

www.ingramcontent.com/pod-product-compliance
Lightning Source LLC
Chambersburg PA
CBHW021813170526
45157CB00007B/2571